The Invisible Generation:

Baby Busters

by George Barna

GEORGE BARNA

THE

INVISIBLE

GENERATION:

Baby Busters

Published by Barna Research Group, Ltd.
647 West Broadway • Glendale, CA 91204-1007

© 1992 by George Barna. All rights reserved.

Printed in the United States. ISBN 1-882297-00-8

ISBN 1-882297-00-8

51800

9 781882 297009

Acknowledgments

THIS BOOK IS THE OUTGROWTH OF THE EFFORTS OF A TEAM of people. Let me thank them at the beginning of this book.

My colleagues at the Barna Research Group, Ltd. have provided me with the support services, the time and the encouragement to complete this task. Thanks Cindy Coats, Keith Deaville, Gwen Ingram, Vibeke Klocke, George Maupin, Paul Rottler, and Ron Sellers.

Paul Rottler used his creative talents to turn the manuscript into a book. Thanks, Paul, for your inventive and tireless efforts to make our information come alive visually.

My wife Nancy and daughter Samantha probably struggled through this process more than anyone else. Thanks, girls, for giving me up days, nights and weekends during the period in which I wrote this. I hope that the impact of the book justifies your sacrifice.

Contents

Three: A Tale of Two Generations
41

Four: You Can't Get There from Here
53

Five: The Heart of the Beast
71

Six: By Their Deeds You Will Know Them
93

Seven: Adventures in the Marketplace
111

Eight: People in Perspective
128

Nine: Tales of Sin, Salvation & Self
151

Ten: Making the Most of the Journey
170

Appendices
179

Preface

WHEN I WAS SEVEN YEARS OLD MY DAYS WERE SPENT reading and memorizing the statistics on the backs of my voluminous set of baseball cards. Life was simple back then. You weeded the garden, got your quarter, marched into the stationary store and purchased two packs of baseball cards, bubble gum intact. Nothing gave me greater pleasure in life than obtaining cards of superstars or of members of the New York Yankees. (In my defense, given the state of the Yankees these days, realize that I was born in that city during an era when being a Yankee was something special.)

I remember one day, after having learned the mathematical formulas for figuring out batting averages, earned runs averages and the like, that I discovered a mistake on one of the cards. I don't remember which player, or what the mistake was, but I sure do remember thinking that I had latched onto something major. Imagine, a mistake on the almighty baseball card! With inextinguishable excitement, I ranted and raved about this discovery of the century to my parents, my younger brother and sister, and my street mates. After a moment or two of intrigue, though, their astonishment waned. Well, maybe it wasn't the Holy Grail I'd just uncovered, but couldn't they see the significance of this new truth?

In retrospect, of course, all of them demonstrated better judgment than I on that occasion.

But the tale does not end there. Few have accused me of being a fast learner. So here we go again, with yet another major discovery I want to share with people, albeit at a different level of significance.

Do you know how much has been written about the Baby Bust generation? Astoundingly little. As a research analyst, I spend hours and hours reading studies, books, magazines, newsletters—anything that seems credible and has some insight into the people who comprise our nation. But with the exception of several subject-specific articles and a single book (concerning Busters as employees), I have found little of any substance about this emerging generation.

So it was with great excitement that I sat down to assemble the information that my company had collected over the past three years which related specifically to the lives of Baby Busters. It was my hope that I would have the privilege of putting this information into a format that would lead many others through a fascinating journey into the minds and hearts of a generation that is virtually unknown.

Throughout this book you will encounter references to various studies conducted by the Barna Research Group. Each of those studies was a nationwide survey conducted by telephone among a random sample of individuals selected via a random-digit sample. (There is a more exhaustive explanation of the methodology in Appendix One of this book.) Other data sources include the Census Bureau and a handful of other research groups whose work we have found to be trustworthy. What you will read is *not* anecdotal in nature because such creative journalism cannot serve as the basis for projectable conclusions about a group of people.

I have, however, included a personal sketch of a Buster at the end of each chapter. These are actual conversations that took place with Busters, outside the course of our quantitative research. The photographs and the names of the people have been changed to protect the identity of those individuals.

I hope that as you read this book and reflect upon your own experiences and relationships with Busters your involvement and potential interaction with them will become more clear and profitable. Frankly, I think Busters grow on you when you get to know them well. And at the risk of overstating the case, can we agree that the Busters, to a significant degree, hold the hope of our nation in their young hands?

Today, my excitement is in being among the first to make this portrait of the Buster generation available to you. But my long-term hope is that by knowing them better, we will be able to build a more pleasant, righteous and productive society.

ONE
Who?

FOR MANY DECADES, SOCIAL ANALYSTS HAVE FOCUSED their trained eyes upon various segments of the population. Using their instincts and available information, sociologists and demographers have woven insightful, fanciful, and sometimes prophetic tales about the growth, lifestyles, values, and aspirations of the myriad of people groups that comprise the American republic.

During the past thirty years, in particular, there has been a special emphasis placed upon the study of *generational* differences. In the Sixties, we heard many analysts wax philosophic, if not sociologic, about the generation gap. A spate of books on the topic was released. In the decades that have followed there has been voluminous attention paid to one particular generation: the Baby Boomers. For a wide variety of reasons, analysts have found the Boomers to be fertile ground for exploration and pontification.

In spite of the growing resources applied to the study of demographic and psychographic changes that are altering the American experience in profound ways, few have ventured into the territory of the Baby Busters.

Who?

Indeed, judging from the conspicuous absence of data, analysis, and interest related to this post-Boomer generation—the millions of Americans who are now coming of age—one must assume that the question "Who?" well summarizes most people's knowledge of the emerging young adult population.

It's a Boomer World, Isn't It?

It's always easier to distill reality in retrospect. Yet, we do know that these days change is happening faster than ever before, and the rules of life seem to shift before our eyes. Those who wish to exploit the changes that are reshaping our world are well-advised to study the values, perspectives, and behaviors of key people groups.

It seems, however, that many who wish to understand and influence the nation have decided that "as the Boomers go, so goes the nation." With that perception firmly embedded in their minds, these individuals lock onto the Boomers as the weather vane generation. Proponents of this approach to societal analysis either tacitly or boldly suggest that if you can comprehend and lead the Boomers, everything else will fall into place. Spending resources on examining other generations is, from this perspective, impractical, and simply a horrid waste of limited resources.

Not So Fast...

As we have begun to explore the world of Baby Busters and to see the world through their eyes, one thing has become clear. Busters are not a generation that is willing to roll over and play dead, allowing the Boomers to call the shots. Busters, in a very different way, are seeking to redesign their environment to create a world which reflects their values, attitudes and dreams.

So who will prevail in this struggle for societal influence and authority? That cannot be foretold at this point. But we can be reasonably sure of one approaching reality: within the next 10 to 15 years, there will be a showdown between the numerous, wealthy, cunning Boomers and their reflective, combative successors, the Busters.

Don't Sell the Busters Short

Are Busters worth studying? Absolutely! Here are just a few of the reasons why they represent a compelling population to examine.

> ➤ *Busters are determined to reshape the nation's prevailing value systems,* which have been virtually rewritten by the Boomers. They view Boomers as possessing twisted perceptions and values; they are vying for a wholesale overthrow of the value systems embraced and nurtured by Boomers. Since values frequently dictate our attitudes, beliefs and behavior, this change of course is of critical importance to those who wish to market products and services, lead government and create public policy, promote religious or lifestyle philosophies, and educate people about our world.

> ➤ *From a purely sociological perspective, Busters comprise a very different breed of Americans* than we have previously witnessed. They were raised differently; they communicate distinctively; their aspirations are unique; they allocate their resources in unique ways; and their numbers position them as a force to be reckoned with. In the power transitions that unfold in the coming decades, their novel views and behaviors will radically recast America and the global politic in which we are a major player.

➤ *As America undergoes a spiritual renaissance of sorts, Busters are leading the charge* to challenge the prevailing notions of what is and is not spiritually significant.

➤ *The Busters are the second largest generation, numerically, America has ever borne.* While the mass media might lead one to assume that Busters are paltry in numbers, there are over 50% more Busters alive today than pre-Boomers. In fact, they constitute about 86% as many individuals as represented by the Boomer generation. This is not a case of statistical deception. Recognize that the Baby Bust population is larger than the entire national population of many nations, including such major, mainstream nations as Canada, Australia, France, England, Spain, Italy, Poland, and Turkey. In fact, *American Busters exceed the national population of all but 11 nations on the face of the earth.*

➤ *The ethnic diversity within the Buster generation is quite substantial.* Among all Busters, 29% are of ethnic minority groups; among the older adults in our population, just 22% are from those ethnic groups.

Given the unique challenges and significance of this generation to marketers, educators, ministers, and policy makers, it is nothing short of amazing that we have all but ignored this generation. Chalk it up to the multifaceted power of the Boomers.

What Is a Baby Buster?

Ask any journalist how to define a Baby Boomer, chronologically, and chances are good that you'll get a consistent response.

Ask those same savvy individuals, however, to enumerate the years during which Baby Busters were born and you're likely to get as many different answers as there are journalists asked. Even sociologists and demographers are at odds when it comes to defining the Busters.

Part of the reason for this dissension, even among the experts, is the matter of whether the Baby Bust is to be described as a true generation (that is, an 18- to 25-year slice of the population) or as a demographic aberration based upon the substantial decline in births after the close of the Baby Boom years.

For our purposes, this book will address the American population as five existing generations, using a generation as a 19-year era. While one can make a strong argument that the very term "Baby Bust" has been derived from the demographic curves, rather than traditional generational sequencing, the phrase is a valuable distinctive for the segment in question.

Terminology

- **Seniors** were born 1926 and earlier
- **Builders** were born 1927 to 1945
- **Boomers** were born 1946 to 1964
- **Busters** were born 1965 to 1983
- 1984 to present are as yet "unnamed"

The oldest generation includes those people we currently refer to as "senior citizens." They are the people born in 1926 or before. Today, they are 66 years of age or older. I'll be calling them the **Seniors.**

The generation that spawned the Baby Boomers consists of adults who are currently 47 to 65 years of age. They were born in the years between 1927 and 1945. Oddly, this generation lacks a consistently-adopted name. In this book, I'll be referring to them as the **Builders.** They were the generation intent upon building a comfortable lifestyle and upon building America into a super-power both economically and militarily. Builders were not satisfied merely to maintain what they inherited. They dedicated themselves and their resources to building a superior life on every front. Indeed, these were the people who elevated to an art form the commitment to give their offspring a better life than they had experienced.

The generation you're probably sick of hearing and reading about is the Baby Boom. Appearing between 1946 and 1964, these were the "war babies"—the 76 million children who were born in the years after World War II and the Korean War. The **Baby Boomers** attained this title because there was such a huge boom in births beginning in 1946 compared to the birth figures for prior years. The Boom years were the first in which more than four million live births occurred. Today the Boomers are 28 to 46 years old, and have an increasingly high and powerful profile in all walks of American society.

Table 1.1

A Definition of the Generations in 1992

Generation	Current Age	Birth Years
Seniors	66+	1926 and earlier
Builders	47 to 65	1927 to 1945
Boomers	28 to 46	1946 to 1964
Busters	**9 to 27**	**1965 to 1983**
adolescents	under 9	1984 to 2002

The **Baby Busters** are known by this title because the era from 1965 through 1983 produced fewer babies per year than were born during the Boom years—i.e. there was a birth bust. As the children of the Boomers, the Baby Bust group has experienced a totally different type of life than any prior generation. Currently 9 to 27 years of age, they have largely been overlooked in public discussion because of the exaggerated attention lavished upon the Boomers.

The youngest generation, one still in the process of formulation, is those people who are 8 years of age and younger. We know little about them, as a generation, and will not be able to begin to reliably analyze and interpret their views and lifestyles for a number of years yet.

"Bust" Is a Misnomer

In comparative terms, the Baby Busters are really not a "bust" generation at all. Put in the larger context, their numbers are actually unusually large, although not as substantial as those witnessed during the Boom years. The figures displayed in Table 1.2 show that in terms of the current population represented by these five generations, the Busters are indeed prolific. While there are nearly 79 million Boomers resident within America today (a three-million person increase in this generation since 1964, due to the influx of immigrants who fall within the Boomer cohort), there are about 68 million Busters. Both of these generations dwarf the Builders (fewer than 44 million) and the Seniors (under 40 million). It appears that the newest generation, which will enter the world between 1984 and 2002, will also be smaller than the Buster group.

Table 1.2
Current Generational Populations

Generation	Millions of People	% of Population
Seniors	39.6	15.9
Builders	43.6	17.5
Boomers	79.0	31.7
Busters	**67.9**	**27.3**
adolescents	18.8	7.6

Numerically, the Boom years were the first in which more than four million new births were recorded in a single year. In fact, the four-million mark was eclipsed eleven times during the Boom years. In contrast, that figure was not reached even once during the Bust years.

However, realize that the average number of babies born during the Bust years was well above average, when compared to the years prior to the Baby Boom. The average number of new births during the Buster years was 3.48 million. The era started out strong, with the most productive year being the first in the 19-year span (1965) when 3.76 million babies were born. The low point was the stretch from 1973 to 1976, when just fewer than 3.2 million newborns entered America each year. The important realization, though, is that *the Bust was a bust only in comparison to the Boom years.*

As a footnote, it is worth mentioning that since the end of the Bust era, the newborn population has again experienced a notable upturn. There have been birth increases each year from 1984 through 1991. The four million mark was reached in 1989 for the first time since the Boom years. (It was exceeded again in 1990 and 1991.) Perhaps this new generation will be known as the Baby Boomlet.

If You've Seen One, You Haven't Seen Them All

One of the undeniable truths about America in the Nineties is that the homogeneity which once characterized us is rapidly dissolving. The ability to predict people's behavior or attitudes based upon ethnic, generational, or historical precedent has been shattered in the last three decades due to the spirit of independence, the new economic realities, the influx of immigrants (both legal and illegal) and the widespread acceptance of what were once viewed as aberrant lifestyles and philosophies.

Three in One

The Baby Bust generation is currently a combination of three distinct segments: those in the 22 to 27 age bracket, those in the 15 to 21 age range, and the 9- to 14-year-olds. There are some areas of values, perspectives, and activities in which these three groups are indistinguishable; and there are other dimensions in which they differ radically. This diversity is, of course, common to all generations, just as the profile of the "typical" Boomer is likely to conflict with the true being of a great many of the Boomers.

Focus on Older Busters

Throughout this book, I will focus primarily upon the views and behavior of the older segments of the Buster population. This is for two primary reasons. First, we know more about them. Second, and more important, the values and behavioral patterns of the older Busters are better established and less likely to change as a natural part of the maturation process. Indeed, while the youngest of the Busters are likely to go through significant lifestyle and attitudinal transitions over the coming decade, the chances are better than average that their perspectives and fundamental values will remain fluid until they ultimately mirror the thoughts and deeds of their older generational colleagues.

BEHIND The Facade

Jeff Bailey ◆ Age: 22

Jeff Bailey is the quintessential Baby Buster. Born in 1970, he was one of two children born to a pair of Boomers in the Northeast. His parents divorced when he was 12, and he and his sister lived with their mother in a series of apartments and condos along the Atlantic coast. His mom lived with *"a regular parade of men; some of them even stayed long enough to remember our names."*

> **"We're kind of an after-thought generation. The spotlight is on the Boomers and the old people. We're basically ignored."**

On occasion, one of these companions would move into their home for an extended stay, bringing along his own brood and thereby creating a temporary blended family. Jeff has few fond memories of these years.

After spending a year in a distant city living with his father and working full-time (*"I needed a break; Dad's place was rent-free and it gave us a chance to spend some time together"*), he is entering his final year of college (*"yeah, I'm pretty typical; I'm doin' the five-year plan"*).

Like so many of his generation, he is a business major and hopes to get into a management position upon graduation. His free time is spent hanging out at campus hot spots with a legion of buddies. Group dating is popular among them. He has no current plans for marriage—nor is he sure that marriage will ever be part of his lifestyle.

Any discussion of Boomers gets him going. *"We labeled 'em 'sociological slime' in my Demography class. Selfish to the bone. Look what they did to the environment. They're money-hungry, self-centered slime buckets. Trouble is, they're everywhere. They just about run the country, man. They sold out their families to get on top, and now they're there."* He shakes his head in disgust and mutters *"Real impressive."*

Although he has studied about Busters, he is only vaguely cognizant of being one. *"We're kind of an after-thought generation. The spotlight is on the Boomers and the old people. We're basically ignored."*

Despite this, he acknowledges a kind of mystical, spiritual unity to his generation. *"We're definitely outnumbered but we have more soul. We have an inner realness that the Boomers never touched. They wanted it all. They thought they got it. Turns out they got the icing but not the cake. We'll get the cake, even if it has already turned bad."*

He underscores the significance of his generation in the historical context. *"Hey, if this country's gonna make it, it won't be because the Boomers rally behind the flag and motherhood, but because we restore some dignity to humanity and some sanity to daily existence. The Boomers have always been willing to sell you down the river to the highest bidder. We're on a different wavelength. Money is important, but it's not the whole picture. We're probably the last hope for creating a sustainable world. Sounds dramatic, I know, but I can't see anyone else out there who's going to say 'hey, that's it, you had your chance, you made a mess of the world, we'll fix it.' It sounds overdone, but most of us really feel this pressure to make things right again. If we blow it, the game's over."*

Two

Who Do They Think They Are?

GETTING TO THE HEART OF WHO THE BABY BUSTERS ARE IS no simple task. While they are perfectly willing to provide a self-analysis, there appear to be aspects about themselves with which they are not comfortable, and other aspects of their character about which they seem ill-informed. The real challenge is to arrive at an accurate understanding of this group based upon a balanced perspective.

To Know Me Is to Love Me

When it comes to personality, nine out of ten Busters describe themselves as outgoing (89%). However, most of them do not feel that they have an aggressive personality (47% say they do). They are comfortable with their level of extroversion, but do not feel that they have crossed the line of rudeness or abrasiveness that they believe characterizes the Boomer generation.

Almost nine out of ten Busters (87%) claim that they are curious by nature. But consistent with their view that they are not overly assertive, more than two-thirds of the Busters (69%) argue that they are easy to please.

Trying to please Busters and successfully persuading or motivating them may be two entirely different matters, though. The experience of many marketers has been that Busters are a group that loves to be entertained. They feel quite at home playing the role of audience, whether it be for a commercial pitch, an artistic event, an athletic contest, or an informational activity.

> **"The proportion of stressed out Busters is nearly double the proportion of older adults who make the same claim."**

But getting this group to act on the desires of the marketer is another story altogether. The Busters admit to this freely, indicating a strong distaste for—and acute awareness of—being manipulated. Even more important is the recognition by a majority of these young adults (57%) that they are skeptics, in general.

The burden of leading a busy life and not feeling able to trust the world has added yet another dimension to the personality of many Busters: stress. Two out of every five Busters (38%) claim they are "stressed out." That represents an extraordinary number of young adults—people who are just starting to get a foothold in life—who already feel the impact of daily pressure in a tangible and impactive manner. The proportion of stressed out Busters is nearly double that of older adults.

Life in the Fast Lane?

Part of the stress recognized by Busters is clearly a response to the fast-paced lives they tend to lead. Nine out of ten Busters (88%) state that they are busy. Half of the generation (47%) goes a step further and admits that they are "too busy." Like the Boomers before them, they are too fascinated by (and drawn to) a world of turbulence and opportunity to reject the temptation to get caught up in the horrific pace. Instead, believing more in their innate ability to control their environment than trusting in their intuition that they will be controlled by their environment, a growing proportion of the Buster generation stays on the daily treadmill, not daring to get off lest they lose out on some special opportunity or "lose their edge."

The emotional and physical fatigue that results from this full-speed-ahead lifestyle is also a partial consequence of the Busters' perception that they work hard. More than nine out of ten Busters described themselves as hard workers (94%). And in the midst of accepting the challenges of life, a surprisingly high proportion of the Busters (47%) think of themselves as being scholarly.

As is often the case for Busters, this emphasis upon the rigorous intellectual evaluation of, and response to, external conditions is intentionally at odds with their perceptions of the Boomers' approach to life. Rather than utilize knee-jerk, self-promoting responses to opportunities—which is how Busters perceive Boomers to react to the world around them—Busters prefer to carefully consider their options and make circumspect choices.

In spite of their reported emphasis upon hard work and a scholarly perspective, few Busters view themselves as being lonely. Just one out of every seven young adults (15%) concluded that they are lonely. Relationships, it turns out, are perceived to be of crucial importance among Busters. While some analysts have chastised the generation for being comparatively less communicative, less expressive, and less relational, the available evidence suggests that Busters have observed the individuality and selfishness of the Boomers and have made a conscious effort to achieve a different kind of human interaction.

Is There Room for God?

In their search for meaning, truth, and success, Busters have consistently sought to understand the Boomer perspective—

and to reject that viewpoint as completely as possible. This attitude is evident in the Buster examination of religion.

Busters are less likely than older adults to describe themselves as "religious." Currently, just over half of the Buster generation see themselves as religious people (52%).

To their credit, most Busters distinguish between being a Christian (using their own definition) and being religious. The vast majority of Busters report at least a nominal Christian upbringing. And their religious character today further reflects such nominalism. Seven out of ten Busters (71%) claim they are Christians. Relatively few Busters claim to be born again, though. While more than four out of ten older adults describe themselves as "born again Christians," only 25% of the Busters assign that label to themselves.

This vague notion of being Christian, but neither overtly religious nor deeply committed to Biblical Christianity, has not precluded most Busters from viewing themselves as leading a traditional lifestyle. Here, as much as any place else, the influence of the Boomer generation can be seen. As Boomers have over the last 20 years steadily redefined what we portray to be traditional or typical, Busters have naively embraced these new views of traditionalism. Even though (as we shall discover in later chapters) Busters are at the leading edge of new family configurations, unique views on world development and personal responsibility, and the practice of entirely original forms of relationships, 71% of the Busters claim they lead a traditional lifestyle.

The Lens of the Buster

Interestingly, it appears that Busters are uncomfortable with terms such as "liberal" and "conservative". Our measurements have found that Busters transition between such descriptive extremes with alarming fluidity. It seems that this is largely attributable to their lack of any societal anchors for the meaning of these terms. In the Sixties and Seventies there were a number of black-and-white issues on which a person's position clearly tagged them as liberal, conservative, progressive, fundamentalist, radical, traditional, or any of a number of other labels. The complexity of issues in the Nineties seems to have removed such clarity. And Busters, sensitive to the shifting winds of political fortune and policy, have expended little energy attempting to position themselves along these anachronistic continuums.

At the same time that they fail to align themselves with the Left or the Right, most Busters do construe themselves to be patriotic (77%). The difference between their response to the Gulf War and that of the Boomers to the Viet Nam War may stand as a case in point. While the circumstances of these two conflicts were clearly different, the underlying attitude and overt response of these generations to the battle of their time paint a clear picture of how they view their world and their responsibility to it.

Interestingly, however, Busters are less likely to describe themselves as patriotic than are Boomers, Builders, or Seniors. More than nine out of ten adults from the older generations claim they are patriotic. This differentiation between the generations may reflect the lost sense of automatic loyalty to institutions, organizations, governments, or other mass entities. With Busters, you receive the fruit of their loyalty once you have earned it. However,

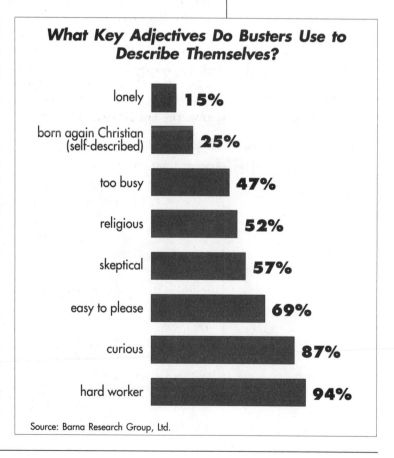

What Key Adjectives Do Busters Use to Describe Themselves?

lonely	15%
born again Christian (self-described)	25%
too busy	47%
religious	52%
skeptical	57%
easy to please	69%
curious	87%
hard worker	94%

Source: Barna Research Group, Ltd.

the process of earning their loyalty never actually ends; it is an enduring, open-ended quest to win them over.

Perhaps surprisingly, most Busters believe they are comfortable financially (68%). What makes this unexpected is that most Busters believe they will never be as well-off financially as their parents and grandparents were. This bleak sense of their financial future has been the cause of some disenchantment and discouragement among Busters. On the other hand, they appear more capable of handling this condition than the Boomers might have been because they do not possess the same value system as the Boomers.

A majority of Busters see themselves as leaders (52%). While this is a high proportion, it is not as high as was witnessed during the same point in the life cycle of the Boomer generation. Nevertheless, the proportion is substantial enough to indicate that the Busters have sufficient chutzpah and aspiration to prepare them for the seemingly inevitable confrontations with the Boomers in the years to come—battles for authority, responsibility, perspective, values, etc.

> "Interestingly, however, Busters are less likely to describe themselves as patriotic than are Boomers, Builders, or Seniors."

Will Busters ultimately satiate their needs as an outgrowth of these approaching inter-generational showdowns? Based on present-day realities, the odds are certainly stacked against them. Many observers question the heart of the Busters to endure a grueling combat with the Boomers. By their own description and admission, the Busters lack the Boomers' obsession with success and leadership; Busters have not committed themselves to building character through achieving spiritual depth; and they seem to lack the emotional stability and endurance to withstand a battle of wills and values.

Busters are neither weak-willed nor ignorant, but neither do they possess the killer instinct of the Boomers. Busters, having lived comfortable (albeit unsatisfying) lives, and being shaped by pessimistic and skeptical views, simply do not seem to have the burning passion for cultural ascendancy that propelled their predecessors to positions of influence and authority at unusually early ages. Their drive seems centered on self-definition and independence.

The Differences Are Evident

If you were to compare the Busters to prior generations with regard to self-perception, glaring differences would emerge. This is true even as we compare the Boomers and Busters, two generations raised with a fairly comparable worldview (e.g. shape the rules to your own needs or liking), relative affluence, and significant opportunities for independence and experimentation.

In comparison to Busters, Boomers emerge as more religious; less stressed out; less difficult to please; less skeptical; less likely to lead a traditional lifestyle; and less likely to see themselves as living comfortably.

Builders and Seniors, when matched against Busters, emerge as more religious; more committed to Christianity; more accepting of people and institutions; less aggressive; less likely to complain of being too busy; and more comfortable with traditional lifestyles.

Different Views of The Same Generation

The differences between Busters and older adults do not end with how they describe themselves. The most significant divergence may be the gap between how Busters view themselves and how they are viewed by their elders.

For instance, studies conducted among employers have shown that Busters are not revered within the labor pool. In fact, a number of employers have become so frustrated by the Buster generation that they have developed innovative strategies for inducing Seniors to remain active employees beyond their normal date of retirement, rather than have to hire and rely upon Busters.

What Are the Gripes against the Busters?

"If you ask a typical young adult to work a hard, eight-hour day, you get laughed at," reported one employer. "The work ethic died around 1965. Today's young people want things handed to them. Paying their dues and earning their way up the ladder are foreign concepts to them."

Another employer offered a similar view. "Prices will have to escalate in the future because I simply will not have as committed or productive a labor force. Employees in their twenties just don't care as much as their predecessors. I'll tell you, you can complain all you want about the selfishness, the driven character, and the greediness of the Baby Boomers, but at least they understood that to get ahead you have to put in a full day's work for a full day's wage. It sure looks like those days are over."

> **"They don't give a damn about what they do, how they do it, or even if they do it. They're more interested in their time off than in what they do while they're on the clock."**

An energetic 63-year-old executive, harboring no thoughts of imminent retirement, stated his views about Busters in characteristically blunt but succinct terms. "They don't give a damn about what they do, how they do it, or even if they do it. They're more interested in their time off than in what they do while they're on the clock. They're worse than their parents. Twenty years ago I never would have thought that would even be possible."

Workplace studies have identified these concerns about the Busters:

➤ they are ambitious, but their ambitions are personal, not corporate;

➤ they are more individualistic, exhibiting little interest in team work or cooperative efforts;

➤ they are uncooperative with authority; they feel a need to make their own decisions, but to leave the consequences of those decisions with the company;

➤ loyalty is not in their vocabulary; it is an "all for one, and one for me" strategy;

➤ they are not driven by desires of excelling in a given career; their career path is generally viewed in a very short-term manner;

➤ their work habits, literacy skills, and training capacity seem less refined than was true for prior generations;

➤ they are not motivated by work; it is a necessary but unappealing means to an end.

Other concerns about the Busters, based on the perceptions of older adults, are that they fear any types of long-term commitment (marriage, friendships, housing, faith, career); they are interested in having a high quality of life but have little interest in working hard to get it; they lack patience; and they are ignorant of the life systems and political processes that they wish to influence to create a different world order. While innately bright, they are seen as a lazy generation and one lacking the drive to excel and innovate.

Nothing They Can Call Their Own

What enables Busters to view themselves so differently than others do? And how can we explain the uniqueness of their profile?

One plausible explanation may be that they are truly a hand-me-down generation. They have not created or embraced much that is uniquely theirs and of which to be proud; they are able to identify little which they believe can be attributed to or possessed solely by their generation. Consider these examples of the cultural habitat.

> ➤ Busters have no heroes. The most commonly mentioned names are recycled heroes from years past, individuals to whom comparatively few Busters really relate. While there are plenty of teen idols and other young entertainment or sports heroes who represent their generation, none of those individuals carries the mantle of trust and credibility of his or her peers.

> ➤ Fashion often helps define or rally a generation. Using clothing to call attention to themselves, their appearance makes a critical statement about who they are and what they represent. Busters have yet to show the fashion flair or novelty that characterized prior generations. If anything, to date they have been more enmeshed in a nostalgic return to past styles than to a focus on the future and creation of a look symbolic of the independence and self-confidence of the generation.

> ➤ Preceding generations championed changed lifestyles. Busters have thus far simply exaggerated the lifestyles of the Boomers. Even though they verbally profess disdain for the lifestyles of the Boomers, today's younger segment has failed to demonstrate innovative, revealing, or unusually significant responses to their environment.

➤ Although the Busters have made a fuss about the vacuous values of the Boomers, they have yet to establish an alternative system of values to replace the Boomer values set. Their tepid explorations of various religious faiths, political ideologies and cultural traditions has not yet resulted in a cutting edge alternative to the heart of the Boomers.

➤ Most generations develop their own sound in popular music. Busters have seen the advent of rap. Predominantly urban, ethnic-driven music, rap has gained popularity among the suburban white masses of Busters. Yet, when asked to claim a musical style that the Busters would proudly embrace as theirs, rap gets less-than-enthusiastic endorsement. Prior generations introduced and stood by the likes of swing, rock, and fusion. The creative talents among the Busters have yet to unleash a compelling sound they can call their own.

Given the absence of a lifestyle, a value system or a world view they can truly claim as their own, the Busters may be suffering from an acute, if low-profile, identity crisis. They have no sense of ownership over their own way of life, and feel less important, if not less mature, as a result.

Thus, it may not be too presumptuous to state that the Busters are still searching for their own place in history, their own sense of self, and their own level of comfort with what they can yet become in a world dominated by the Boomers.

BEHIND *The Facade*

Tony Esperanza ◆ Age: 19

"Man, I blew off work today," Tony crows to his three male companions as they sit awkwardly on the curb outside the local 7-11. *"Too boring, man. There's more to life than studyin' and workin' all the time."*

A high-five from one of his buddies seals the truth of the statement in their minds.

Tony comes from a second-generation Hispanic family. His parents came to the southwest from Mexico some 18 years earlier. While he was born in Mexico, he has no memories of his native land. All he really knows is America. He speaks both English and Spanish fluently, although his grades in school suggest that he has never taken the formalities of either language too seriously.

Pushed by his parents, Tony is enrolled in a local community college, working slowly toward an Associate's degree in one of the social sciences (he hasn't decided which one yet). He works full-time at a nearby shoe store, serving *"fat ladies who swear they take a size 6 when their feet swear they need a size 7."* A jovial person, he likes the interaction with the customers, but does not take the job seriously.

"It's just a way of getting the money to pay the bills and maybe save a dollar or two for a new car."

The weight of the world is on his shoulders, the way he tells the story. Forty hours of work each week. Twenty hours of classes and homework. Time for the family. Time for his female friends. Time with the guys. How can *anyone* balance such a

> **"The weight of the world is on his shoulders, the way he tells the story."**

full portfolio, he constantly wonders. No wonder he feels plagued by stress even before his twentieth birthday.

His joy in life, though, is the time he spends with people. Like so many in his generation, he likes talking about life and values with a wide array of individuals—even if he is not yet clear what he, personally, believes.

"Yeah, you hear a lot of different views when you work in a cultural crossroads like this area. But that's what makes it fun, too. You always have a new perspective to think about...some new ideas. Hey, I'm still young, I've still got some time to figure out who I am. I like learning about the journey other people have been on."

Tony's view of himself is sometimes at odds with the view that others possess of him. At work, for instance, he has been written up by his supervisor for wasting time. He has a ready reply.

"Man, they don't know how good they have it by having me as an employee. I never call in sick. I'm always on time. I don't give the customers a hard time; they like me. Sometimes, you get tired. It's not easy keeping these ladies satisfied. So what do they write me up for? Bad rap, man, bad. They're lucky they have someone like me."

If the opportunity arose, Tony would not even consider remaining at the store in a management position. He may not know what he wants out of life, but he can certainly identify some things he does not want—and retail sales is one of them.

"I like to learn about a lot of things. I like to travel. I enjoy new experiences. This job won't ever give me what I'm looking for."

And what exactly is that?

"I don't know. Maybe a good living, the chance to run things and make important decisions, a chance to have some flexibility in life. I don't want to get tied down too fast, you know?"

Reebok said it: "Life is short; play hard."

THREE

A Tale of Two Generations

A TESTIMONY TO OUR NATIONAL INFATUATION WITH THE Boomers is the fact that we now evaluate all other generations in comparison to the Boomers. That post-war generation has risen to become the cultural yardstick by which we measure all other groups.

This reality angers the Busters. They view this as insulting and as a reason underlying their own loss of identity and prominence. This condition also highlights the vast differences in history, present circumstances, and likely futures between the Busters and Boomers.

Where They've Come From

Boomers will not have the opportunity to tell the tales frequently recalled by their own parents—walking miles to school every day, waking at the break of dawn to shovel snow, spending hours cutting firewood for the family furnace, rotating the same three sets of clothing for the entire school year, being thrilled to get a full-time job for just a few dollars a week, and so on.

The Builders revel in such stories because it reminds them of the success they have achieved through their own toil and sweat. In general, there were few Builders who were "born with a silver spoon in their mouth"; what they got, they earned.

Boomers, however, had it much easier. They were the offspring of the parents who made "I want to give my child a better life than I had" a dominant credo. In many ways, the Boomers served as a transitional generation. Consider some of the changes related to the Boomers.

➤ They were the generation for which the decline in household size became both consistent and statistically significant.

➤ They were the first generation for which a majority did not have to worry about economic survival, but could instead concentrate upon economic expansion.

➤ It was not until the Boomers arrived that attaining a college degree or a full-time job became common for women.

➤ With the widespread availability of technological conveniences—telephones, television sets, automobiles—Boomers grew up in a more comfortable environment, one in which mass communications were more prolific, and leisure transitioned from a privilege to an expectation.

➤ Suddenly, to be part of the "working class" was to be looked down upon. Formerly viewed as the backbone of the nation's economy and the true champions of the national spirit, blue collar workers rapidly gained a reputation for being mere commoners rather than members of the upwardly mobile elite.

Busters are a generation for which the transition continues, but in some new and unexpected ways. They have continued some of the transformations which made the Boomers so unique, but have rejected other changes and put their own twist on contemporary lifestyles and perspectives.

Head to Head

In a direct comparison, here's how the Boomers and Busters differ in terms of background, behavior and viewpoint.

Sense of History

Boomers grew up in an era when traditional family values were still cherished by adults. Rules and traditions were meaningful, although less frequently adhered to than in prior days.

Busters grew up living in the shadow of their rebellious parents. Consequently, theirs was much more likely to be an unconventional upbringing. Even though they are aware of traditional family configurations and conventional rules, these elements have seemed irrelevant to the contemporary life. And whatever clarity of values existed for the Boomers, that wisdom has become ambiguous for the Busters.

Ideals

Boomers were idealistic, believing that people were basically good and that the world was worth saving and improving. Boomers have a very practical side to them, but they have concurrently grasped the importance and skill of dreaming big and striving for the dream.

Busters, in comparison, are less confident in people and institutions. Consequently, they are more opportunistic. They will pursue the pragmatic before the idealistic. They are not sure it is possible to save the world, and their primary reason for doing so would be based mostly upon the desire to survive, rather than any type of warm and fuzzy emotionalism.

Directing the Future

Boomers believed that the future was waiting to be created. They were optimistic about the future. They were anxious to experiment with innovative approaches. Part of the joy of life was to take risks and see what would happen. The fear of failure was not a paralytic agent.

Busters are world-class skeptics, cynical about mankind and pessimistic about the future. They have focused upon coping with a global reality that is, in their eyes, neither enviable nor redeemable. The key skill is not innovation but adaptation.

Expectations

Boomers felt they were special people and were entitled to the best the world had to offer.

"Busters are world-class skeptics, cynical about mankind and pessimistic about the future."

Busters feel as if they have been forgotten, if not intentionally limited. They are ambivalent about the future, just as they feel that society is ambivalent about them. They would like to get, and would probably appreciate getting, the best. Yet, realistic as they are, their sights are set somewhat lower.

Stability and Change

Boomers grew up accepting the possibility of change. Their focus was upon allowing reasonable change, but ultimately seeking stability. Progress, in their eyes, represented a careful balance between exploring the unknown and sticking with the tried-and-true. Emotionally, they struggled with the competing interests of the novel and the predictable.

Busters have grown up only knowing change. Thus, their lives are dominated by the persistence of change, with their dominant desire being to exert greater influence over the changes that are created around them. Their definition of success has been greatly tinted by their assumption that life revolves around the management and manipulation of constant transitions toward a more perfect evolution.

Integrating Information

Boomers matured in a period when information was highly valued but a difficult commodity to obtain. Many Boomers devoted their lives to getting treasured factual data as a basis for innovations. Access to, and the application of, critical information comprised a fast track to power and wealth.

> **"Busters view education as a necessary evil. Their thrust is to gain whatever knowledge they must have to get by in life."**

Busters have grown up during the information explosion. Information has been readily available; consequently, it is no longer a cherished commodity but an integral fact of life. The sense of awe over the volume of available information, the feeling of astonishment over the power of empirical wisdom, and the appreciation for the meaning of a life sans hard, deep data have been absent from the Buster world view. And they behave accordingly.

Hitting the Books

Boomers were rebellious, but remained convinced of the value of education. They reshaped that education to meet their own needs, blending traditional schooling emphases with personal preferences in light of their idealism. Learning remained a process of discovery, possessing inherent value.

Busters view education as a necessary evil. Their thrust is to gain whatever knowledge they must have to get by in life. College is viewed as a right rather than a privilege; in fact, many think of it as an irrelevant but necessary credential toward getting their fair share of power and money. Boomers turned their backs on the classics; Busters have turned theirs on any type of intellectually or spiritually challenging reading.

Nine-to-five

Boomers have seen work as an end in itself. Doing a good job and getting ahead in the marketplace have been driving forces in their lives. A significant portion of their identity came from their status and performance on the job.

Busters view work as a means to an end. Their commitments to long hours, climbing the corporate ladder, and gaining their self-image and prestige through employment success are noticeably diminished compared to that of their predecessors.

Dollars and Cents

Boomers have experienced unparalleled economic expansion. They believe that the sky is the limit if one is willing to work hard, think big, and experience a bit of luck.

Busters expect to experience economic parity or decline in comparison with their parents. They view the world as offering them less of a chance to get ahead and believe that such a determined drive to succeed financially is not worth the price paid to gain such riches. Workaholism—a widespread disease among the Boomers—is unlikely to reach epidemic proportions among the younger adults.

Success Defined

Boomers defined economic success as achieving greater wealth and prosperity than any prior generation had ever experienced.

Busters define economic success as achieving levels of wealth commensurate to that reached by their parents.

Self-concept

Boomers have remained an abundantly self-indulgent, bold, and aggressive lot. They will not accept "no" for an answer. They view the world as theirs to exploit—and they go for it with unbridled enthusiasm and energy.

Busters have always felt inferior. While they, too, tend to be selfish and unyielding on principles, their principles are different. They are more apt to be protective of what they have, and to whine about what they don't have.

Bonds of Friendship

Boomers valued relationships, but built them in new ways. Their interaction has been based on constant negotiation, and the belief that transient relationships are no less acceptable or valuable than any other form of relationship. Boomers were the original networkers, a concept that fits well with their utilitarian view of life and people.

Busters have outright rejected the impersonal, short-term, fluid relational character of their parents.

> **"What emerges are two generations bonded by blood, but separated by emotion and expectation."**

They have veered more toward traditional, longer-term relationships. However, given their cynicism and pessimism, they have also lowered their expectations vis-a-vis relationships: their potential duration, the number of significant bonds, and their fervor to create a wide pool of contacts. Boomers sought relational breadth; Busters seek relational depth.

What emerges are two generations bonded by blood, but separated by emotion and expectation. There also remains the possibility that Busters, as they mature, will slowly embrace more and more of the qualities of their parents' generation. But given their vastly divergent views of life, the probability of such a smoothing process is limited.

The View Depends on the Angle

Boomers are not the only yardstick against which a generation can be measured. And, of course, there is nothing to suggest that how people view the Busters is any more significant than how the Busters view others.

Consider this alternative angle on inter-generational views. Based on the accumulated research, here's how each of the last three generations views its counterparts.

➤ Builders think of the Boomers as disrespectful, overly blunt, greedy, possessing warped values, and leading unbalanced lives. They envy their education, their mastery of technology, and their drive for leadership.

➤ Builders think of Busters as unusually immature, impatient, lacking a sense of ethics or morality, lazy, meddling, and emotionally unstable. Yet, they are hopeful that Busters will arrive at a thoughtful alternative values system to that of the Boomers. It is assured that they are "off to a slow start," but may turn out better for it.

➤ Boomers view Builders as rigid and inflexible, old-fashioned, too cautious for their own good, predictable, and generally out of touch with the real world. Concurrently, they respect their consistency, their pioneering spirit, and are intrigued by their traditional ethics and morality.

➤ Boomers view Busters as selfish and impertinent, manipulative, aloof, passionless, and lacking in marketable skills and insights. Then again, they see a lot of themselves in this younger segment and hope to fine tune some of the "errant views" they now possess.

➤ Busters perceive Builders to be unwilling to change, wise but anachronistic, more excited about history than the future, and boring to be around. Many Busters also appreciate what the Builders were able to do to overcome the barriers of their day. The few heroes of the Buster tend to be from the Builder generation.

➤ Busters think of Boomers as workaholics, too superficial, selfish, unidimensional, impersonal, uncaring, and unrealistic. They acknowledge that Boomers had the guts to challenge the system; that they have made the world a more interesting (albeit confusing) place; and they share a similar passion for excellence, for quality leisure time, and for the chance to create rather than inherit a pre-determined future.

B E H I N D *The Facade*

Richard and Robert Marx ◆ Ages: 31 & 20

Meet Rich and Rob. They are brothers. Talking with them opens new vistas of generational understanding. Rich is a Boomer, 31 years old. Rob is the Buster in the family, having just turned 20. And they couldn't be more aptly named: Rich, the Boomer, feels as if life is waiting to shower him with its rewards. Rob, the Buster, argues passionately that not only isn't life fair, but his generation has been robbed of compelling reasons to live.

> **"They don't take chances. They want it all handed to them. Sometimes I get depressed thinking that they are the future of our country."**

Rich, on the Busters: *"Don't get me wrong; I love my brother. But—and we've talked about this, no, **argued** is more like it, for hours on end—he just doesn't get it. People his age just do not comprehend what life is about and how to make the most of it. They operate scared. They don't take chances. They want it all handed to them. Sometimes I get depressed thinking that they are the future of our country."*

Rob, on the Boomers: *"Boomers are just such cultural snobs. They slam us for not making environmentalism our issue; meanwhile, they're devoting their energy to making bucks off the system that spoiled it in the first place. They say that the world offers more opportunities than ever these days. Yeah? By the time they're through raping the universe, there's not much of anything left for anybody.*

They claim we don't have the drive and the ability to get ahead in a global world. Easy to complain when you never had to take on the same challenge."

Rich thinks the problem is attitudinal. *"We grew up with a ton of adversities. But we simply rolled over them and made our stands. Younger adults today just bitch and moan about how much tougher it is today. It's no tougher. They have more resources, more opportunities. Everything is relative."*

Rob thinks the problem is the Boomers. *"They're pulling a Cain and Abel deal on us. They're totally swiping the inheritance from us. Can we get ahead in the world today? Not unless they'll let us take a meaningful part in the proceedings. Instead, they're freezing us out."*

How do you get ahead, then, in life these days?

"You work your butt off and then analyze your strategy and payout, regroup, and go for it again. Smart, hard work," proclaims Rich. *"Simple and easy as that."*

"Try to hold on to what you've got," says Rob. *"And keep probing for new, untapped opportunities that will give you a deeper foothold on the society. You cannot get locked into any one course of action or way of thinking over the long haul. Flexibility is central to survival these days. And that's really the key: just plain surviving the ordeals of daily life."*

FOUR

You Can't Get There from Here

MOST AMERICANS DID NOT GROW UP WITH THE DISHEART-ening feeling that they will never be able to achieve their dreams. But that is how most Baby Busters feel: surprisingly hopeless in a world seen by their elders as possessing virtually unparalleled opportunity.

The disparity between the expectations of Busters and other generations is apparent in many ways. The generations identify the problems of their world differently; they define their personal issues and obstacles differently; and they describe their expectations for the years to come in very different terms.

The Uphill Personal Battle

Americans have always been unusually optimistic about the future. However, Busters are the first generation in the past 60 years (i.e. since such estimates have been available) to believe their future will not exceed or even match the experiences of their parents' generation.

In fact, research we conducted in 1992 showed that Busters were four times more likely to indicate that the quality of their life had deteriorated in the past 12 months than to suggest that it had improved. And they were not terribly hopeful about the future; one-third said they expect the quality of their life to decline even further.

Busters clearly differ from older adults when it comes to the issue agenda that wins their attention and resources. Older adults, because of their greater degrees of fiscal stability and personal achievement, identify their most pressing personal issues as those which they cannot readily control. Maintaining or regaining peak physical health, for instance, looms as a larger issue for Builders and Seniors than for either of the younger generations. Mastering family challenges is another significant matter for Boomers and Builders. Avoidance of, or protection from, crime also stand as major objectives to pre-Buster generations, both because older adults feel more physically vulnerable and because they have a greater storehouse of materials to guard.

Busters frame their life issues in terms of what it takes to get a foothold in the world. This is perhaps more of a reflection of their stage in life than it is a distinctive of their generation based on a radically different world view. For instance, the three most challenging personal issues for Busters are overcoming their immediate financial needs (mentioned by 27% of this segment); achieving success in their career (noted by 26%); and satisfactorily completing their education (23%).

To round out the picture, consider the issues that are not even on the agenda in the typical Buster mind. Handling crimes against the individual is deemed a very important personal issue for just 2%. Likewise, achieving and maintaining good health is a key issue to only 2%. Coping with substance abuse was a critical matter to 7%. And while older adults rail about the anxieties created by the time pressures and fast pace of life among the Busters, it is at best a handful of the Busters themselves who cite time pressures as a major personal difficulty (4%).

Lodged somewhere in between these two ends of the issue-significance continuum is the matter of relationships and personal social obligations. Overall, about one in eight Busters claims that the development and maintenance of friendships and social contacts is a major concern in their life. About one in eight Busters identified relationships and social challenges as a major personal issue.

Table 4.1
The Personal Issues Considered by Busters to be Most Significant

description of issue area	mentioned by
personal financial problems	27%
career/job pressures, challenges	26
completion/furthering of education	23
family-related challenges	14
relationships and social difficulties	12
coping with substance abuse	7
overcoming transportation problems	5
handling time pressures	4
fear of crime	2

(NOTE: all answers were to an open-ended question; respondents were allowed to provide multiple answers, resulting in percentages adding to greater than 100%.)

Source: Barna Research Group, Ltd.

Seemingly more than the generations that preceded them, Busters are having difficulty sorting out the relational character of their lives. They are clear in their rejection of the *laissez-faire*, utilitarian approach to relationships taken by the Boomers. They are not enamored of the time-intensive approach that characterized the interactions of Builders and Seniors. Yet, as they have searched for a pleasing means of relating to others, they have failed to find a satisfying alternative. While they value relationships, they remain undecided as to the number, depth, and nature of "successful" relationships they seek to foster.

The World as Busters View It

Even the global perspective of Busters differs from that of their elders.

Table 4.2

National and International Issues Considered by Busters to be Most Significant

description of issue area	mentioned by
substance abuse	34%
world stability	31
reducing/eliminating the national debt	20
establishing strong environmental protection policies	16
abortion rights	14
addressing poverty	7
fear of/protection from crime	6
the AIDS epidemic	6
reducing the defense budget	6
improving public education	5
family difficulties	3
financial stress and challenges	3
deterioration of morality and values	1
absence of religious faith	1
transportation policies and systems	1

(NOTE: all answers were to an open-ended question; respondents were allowed to provide multiple answers, resulting in percentages adding to greater than 100%.)

Source: Barna Research Group, Ltd.

Recent research on the socio-political views of Busters finds them to be more inclined to focus on domestic policies and problems than upon international concerns. The statistics also point out that Busters are primarily concerned with those issues which have the highest potential to affect them personally, as opposed to demonstrating an altruistic concern for those affairs which will have the most encompassing impact.

Five issues were identified by at least 10% of the Busters as representing major concerns. The most commonly mentioned were substance abuse (34%); world peace and stability (31%); economic solvency and the national debt (20%); environmental protection and restoration (16%); and abortion (14%).

Equally surprising were some of the issues that were not deemed of major concern to Busters. Poverty was a major issue to just 7%; crime to only 6%; family difficulties and transitions, mentioned by 3%; deterioration of morality, 1%; and the absence of religious involvement 1%.

Notice the differences and similarities between the most vexing issues personally, and those which Busters view as being the most societally pressing concerns. For instance, while relatively few Busters believe that they or a close personal friend struggle with substance abuse, this issue emerges as one of those which they construe to be of major national proportions. Family matters loom large on the personal agenda for Busters, yet few of them see family issues as something that plagues the nation at large.

> **"Busters are primarily concerned with those issues that have the highest potential to affect them personally, as opposed to demonstrating an altruistic concern for those affairs which will have the most encompassing impact."**

On the other hand, issues such as crime seem to be neither personally troubling nor a dominant national problem from the Buster perspective. The fact that older adults identify crime as one of the leading issues requiring our attention may reflect the disparate economic status levels of the generations.

A similarly unique view of the world comes through upon examining the social and political issues that Busters say would inform their choice of presidential candidate. Asked to rate the importance of a candidate's stands on each of fifteen issues in their choice of a candidate, Busters clearly distinguished themselves from their elders. Tops on the Busters' list of important indicators were candidates' stands on public education and the national economy. The next highest echelon of critical issues included positions on crime, the enforcement of drug laws, health care, and environmental policy.

Table 4.3

Issues Considered by Busters to be Very or Somewhat Important in the Selection of a President

(Asked Only of Registered Voters)

issue	percent
health care	99%
national economy	99
public education	99
human rights protection	98
budget deficit	95
drug law enforcement	95
taxes	95
crime	93
environmental policy	93
women's rights	93
welfare and unemployment	90
military and defense spending	86
abortion	84
separation of church and state	81
mass transportation	74

Source: Barna Research Group, Ltd.

By way of comparison, note that the most compelling issues in the minds of Boomers, Builders, and Seniors were somewhat different.

Table 4.4

Proportion of Adults Who Say An Issue Is Very Important in Their Selection of a Presidential Candidate

Issue	Busters	Boomers	Builders	Seniors
• women's rights	48%	50%	47%	52%
• abortion	53	55	57	57
• taxes	60	64	71	69
• environmental policy	67	58	53	57
• public education	80	79	77	77
• crime	69	74	79	87
• military and defense spending	53	48	48	63
• budget deficit	55	60	68	71
• health care	67	74	79	80
• welfare and unemployment policies	52	62	67	64
• separation of church and state	38	44	61	53
• drug law enforcement	70	76	81	87
• human rights protection	58	63	70	73
• the economy	76	73	82	76
• mass transportation	15	20	28	40

Source: Barna Research Group, Ltd.

Among Boomers the top-ranked issues were public education and enforcement of the drug laws, followed closely by health care provision, crime, and enhancing the economy.

Builders were most concerned about crime, the economy, enforcement of drug laws, and health care.

Seniors stressed the importance of a candidate's commitment to dealing with crime, health care, and enforcement of our drug laws.

Notice that in comparison to the other age groups, Busters exhibit the highest level of concern for just one issue: environmental policy. They more commonly exhibit the lowest degree about issues, as is the case related to taxes, crime, the budget deficit, health care, welfare policy, church and state separation, human rights protection, and mass transportation policies.

The Impossible Dream, Reprise

The Busters also have a unique definition of what they deem desirable in life. Their ideal scenario includes some elements that are not currently a source of anxiety (because they take those aspects for granted); some elements to which they aspire and about which they remain hopeful; and some aspects which they either do not foresee (and have therefore given up on) or in which they have little interest.

By far the most desirable life circumstance, among the 13 aspects which we tested, is having good health. Nine out of ten Busters said good health is a very desirable condition for their life. This was similar to the response provided by other adults. It is also one of the realities which most Busters currently accept to be a given: they have good health and they expect it to continue.

The life conditions deemed considerably more desirable by Busters than by older adults were having close friendships with people; having a high-paying job; exerting influence in the lives of other people; owning a large home; achieving some measure of fame or public recognition; and living comfortably.

The unifying thread running through these elements is material achievement and influence. Again, whether this is a consequence of their current status as new to the job market or

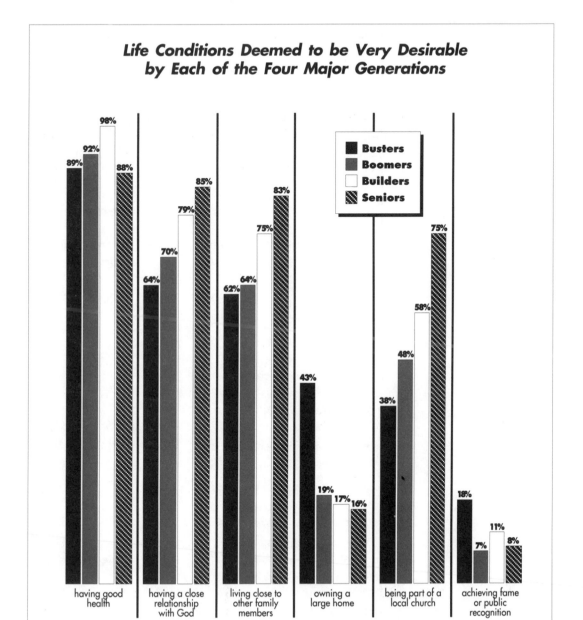

Life Conditions Deemed to be Very Desirable by Each of the Four Major Generations

Legend: Busters, Boomers, Builders, Seniors

having good health: 89%, 92%, 98%, 88%

having a close relationship with God: 64%, 70%, 79%, 85%

living close to other family members: 62%, 64%, 75%, 83%

owning a large home: 43%, 19%, 17%, 16%

being part of a local church: 38%, 48%, 58%, 75%

achieving fame or public recognition: 18%, 7%, 11%, 8%

Source: Barna Research Group, Ltd.

reflective of real differences in world view remains to be seen. Other differences worthy of note are the lower levels of interest ascribed to being part of a local church, having a close relationship with God, and being known as a person of integrity. These were the elements that related more to the moral character of the individual. Clearly, these are not of high interest to Busters in comparison to the views and desires of older adults.

Table 4.5

Life Conditions Deemed to be Very Desirable by Each of the Four Major Generations

life condition described	Busters	Boomers	Builders	Seniors
• having good health	89%	92%	98%	88%
• having close personal friendships	80	69	75	83
• living comfortably	69	53	59	76
• being known as a person of integrity	65	79	79	70
• having a close relationship with God	64	70	79	85
• living close to other family members	62	64	75	83
• having a high paying job	56	34	27	15
• living to an old age	55	48	48	61
• owning a large home	43	19	17	16
• having an influence on other peoples' lives	49	39	38	33
• being part of a local church	38	48	58	75
• not having to work for a living	30	33	38	41
• achieving fame or public recognition	18	7	11	8

Source: Barna Research Group, Ltd.

Perhaps you noticed that Busters are closest in their perspectives to Boomers on some items, closest to the views of Builders on a few, and nearly identical to the Seniors on still other matters.

This unpredictable pattern is further evidence of a generation in transition. The Busters are a people group searching for a unique identity in the context of tried and true historical responses by the generations that preceded them. In all likelihood, the end result will be a unique mixing and matching of tried and untried philosophies, behaviors, and viewpoints that will move the Busters toward realizing their ultimate goals.

> **"The Busters are a people group searching for a unique identity in the context of tried and true historical responses by the generations that preceded them."**

One Day at a Time

The expectations for the future are, indeed, bleak in the eyes of the Busters. Their assumptions about the coming decade underscore the sense of pessimism they bring to the debate.

When it comes to economics, Busters are downright chagrined. Traditionally, Americans have assumed that as technology evolves and America increases its domination of the world economic scene, adults will be able to live in heightened prosperity while working fewer hours. However, only one out of six Busters believes that by the year 2000 people will be working fewer hours each week. They assume that to remain on an even footing with their current lifestyle they will have to work more hours.

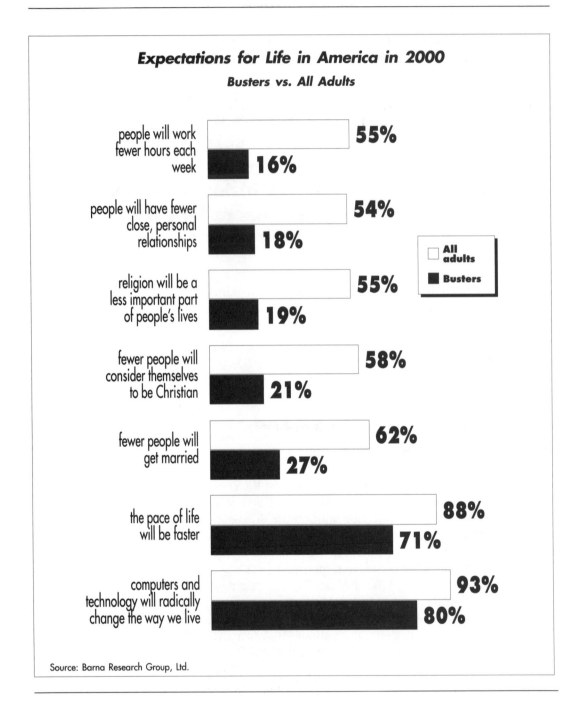

Expectations for Life in America in 2000
Busters vs. All Adults

people will work fewer hours each week
- All adults: **55%**
- Busters: **16%**

people will have fewer close, personal relationships
- All adults: **54%**
- Busters: **18%**

religion will be a less important part of people's lives
- All adults: **55%**
- Busters: **19%**

fewer people will consider themselves to be Christian
- All adults: **58%**
- Busters: **21%**

fewer people will get married
- All adults: **62%**
- Busters: **27%**

the pace of life will be faster
- All adults: **88%**
- Busters: **71%**

computers and technology will radically change the way we live
- All adults: **93%**
- Busters: **80%**

☐ All adults
■ Busters

Source: Barna Research Group, Ltd.

No Brighter Tomorrows

Busters reject the conventional notion that the future will bring better times for all. The typical American view is that if we continue to produce goods and to pursue progress in life systems, people's lives will continually improve. Just one-fifth of the Busters, though, buy this line of reasoning. Most Busters do not believe that there will be fewer poor people, or that Americans will be significantly wealthier in the coming years. While they expect greater numbers of people to receive a college education, they dismiss the long-held assumption that there exists an ironclad connection between a college degree and economic ascendance. In fact, increasing numbers of Busters admit to entertaining thoughts about their own prospects of winding up in poverty.

A Changing Perception of Christianity

Most Americans (more than four out of five) consider themselves to be "Christian." Over the last several decades, that faith label has taken on a pale image of its past meaning. Today, most self-described Christians would be nominal Christians, at best, given their failure to participate in organized religious activities, personal spiritual development, or to study or understand the basic components of a Biblical faith. Most adults foresee an America which becomes increasingly pluralistic in its religious views and behavior.

Perhaps surprisingly, Busters are the generation that is least likely to predict the worst for the Christian faith in America. Only one-fifth of the Busters believe that fewer people will consider themselves to be Christian by the turn of the decade. That is about one-third as many as make the same prediction among older adults. Further, Busters were only one-third as likely as their elders to state that religion will become less important in people's lives.

The reason for this surprising conclusion probably has to do with the Busters' context for interpreting life. Most Seniors and

Builders not only professed to be Christians but overtly invested themselves in their faith. Boomers ruptured the trend line by not only questioning the veracity and value of organized religion and Christianity, in particular, but by distancing themselves from the practice of their beliefs.

Table 4.6

Expectations for Life in America in 2000

expected condition	Busters	all adults
• computers and technology will radically change the way we live	80%	93%
• the pace of life will be faster	71	88
• people will do more of their shopping by mail, telephone, computer, and means other than physically visiting a store	56	85
• the majority of adults will have a college education	44	69
• there will be increased incidents of lying, stealing and cheating	33	71
• fewer people will get married	27	62
• fewer people will consider themselves to be Christian, or to associate with some type of Christian church	21	58
• there will be fewer homeless or poor people	19	39
• religion will be a less important part of people's lives	19	55
• people will have fewer close, personal relationships	18	54
• Americans will be significantly wealthier than they are today	17	43
• people will work fewer hours each week	16	55

Source: Barna Research Group, Ltd.

Exposed primarily to the religious views and behaviors of the Boomers, Busters have a different context for understanding Christianity. Their view of Christianity, Boomer-style, is a faith that is superficial, manipulative, convenient, and theologically ambiguous. Given this decidedly Nineties view of Christianity, it is not so astonishing to discover that Busters foresee this attenuated form of Christianity will maintain its place in American culture.

Consistent with their expectation that religion and Christianity will remain a core dimension of the national character, Busters also expressed relatively greater optimism that people's moral character will not deteriorate; that personal relationships will thrive; and that marriage as a social institution will survive. All of this, in their eyes, in a society in which the pace of life continues to increase, and technology will radically restructure the nature of our existence.

Breaking the Mold

Busters, then, maintain an odd mixture of pessimism about their personal economic potential with optimism about their relational possibilities and the likely moral and spiritual character of the nation.

What may be most stressful to Busters, though, is the realization that the world in which they live is so much more complex than the environment in which any prior generation was raised. The immediate implication is that if the world is going to reflect the positive qualities which they cherish or hope will prevail, then Busters themselves cannot passively await the development of such attributes. They must aggressively seek to guide the development of the nation in line with their own views and dreams.

This will not be an easy task for the Busters, since they are not big risk-takers—certainly not as daring as the Boomers. The extent to which they strive to make America embrace the perspectives and values they hold dear will greatly determine their fulfillment with, and willingness to contribute to, American culture in the twenty-first century.

BEHIND
The Facade

Curtis Farmington ◆ Age: 25

The story of Curtis Farmington may not be typical, but it is reflective of the troubled minds of many Busters. Curtis, born and bred in Washington, D.C., worked hard to get into a top-notch college. He studied hard while on campus but eventually found that the pressures and temptations were too much for him. A three-year drug habit ensued, until his family and friends helped him get clean through a residential rehab program. Today, he lives with his family and works as a law clerk while taking evening courses in a law program.

His drug problems have indelibly colored his view of the world.

> **"His drug problems have indelibly colored his view of the world."**

"There are many opportunities out there for young, aggressive people like me. But there are a multitude of traps, too. Even the opportunities are not as stupendous as they were, say, five or ten years ago. The world is getting smaller, and we're watching 'progress' dry up some of the chances we might have had to get ahead."

His focus these days is totally career-driven. His conversations invariably return to a small set of familiar themes: finishing his law degree; living with his parents until he can make it on his own; avoiding the temptations to fall back into the lazy relational and lifestyle patterns that led to his drug use; the desire to use his legal training to tackle some of the world's ills.

He is a registered voter and has opinions about the system, but is not terribly impressed with, or excited about any of the major candidates running for the presidency. He criticizes their lack of substance. He gamely states that he will vote in November, but is not enthusiastic about the ballot options.

Why seek a law degree in a nation that is already glutted with lawyers?

"Getting a Bachelor's degree isn't enough anymore. Everyone gets a grad degree nowadays. Why law? It's where the action is. I can't see myself doing a 9-to-5 for forty years, making widgets or punching a computer keyboard. Life is what you make it. It's harder to make something of it these days, but if you really commit yourself to a better future, you can probably score at least part of your dream."

The Heart of the Beast

TO TRULY UNDERSTAND A GROUP OF PEOPLE, THE MOST IN-sightful information is that which reveals their values. From the core values spring forth attitudes, morals, and behavior. While we sometimes act inconsistently with our values (most often during a period of transition from one value set to another), our behavior is the clearest reflection of what we hold dear.

Here's What's Important

For Busters, like the rest of the nation, the early Nineties are a time of re-examination and re-evaluation of their values. After the emotional roller coaster ride through the Seventies and Eighties, and in the midst of the swirling lifestyle changes wrought by new technologies and global restructuring, most adults are rethinking their priorities in life. This is no less true for the Busters, although their process is different because they had not yet developed a value system with which they were satisfied. Thus, for Boomers, Builders, and Seniors, the process is about refining those values. For the Busters, the quest to define them remains central.

In the current scheme of things, Busters concur with their elders that the things they rate as the most important elements in life are their family and their health. While other priorities are shifting, these two have remained stable and entrenched at the top of the list.

After these factors, though, some telling generational distinctions emerge. For instance, Busters place a much higher premium upon the importance of career and money. At the same time, they downplay the importance of religion, the Bible, and their free time. The relatively depressed levels of importance assigned to religion and the Bible are particularly significant given the aimlessness of much of the generation (i.e. their search for meaning and truth) and the concurrent growth in religious exploration among the remainder of the population.

> **"These days the pressure to pursue and achieve is in place well before graduating from school."**

Realize that a majority of Busters cite religion and the Bible as very important in their life. However, when placed in the context of the other elements they deem to be very important, religion and the Bible reside on the lower end of the scale. The same contextual relationship is true regarding their friendships.

The differences between Busters and older adults should not obscure the ranking of the Busters' priorities, for this, too, reveals something of their character and life perspective. After family and health, the ranking values are time, career, and friends. The lofty rating of these factors are indicative of the greater relational bent of Busters and their sensitivity to the worth of their time. Life is not, as in generations past, a comparatively carefree, slowly building climb to the top for a young adult. These days the pressure to pursue and achieve is in place well before graduating from school.

Notice that despite their focus upon achievement and progress, money, as a pure goal, does not rank as high as might be expected. Perhaps this is partly because they understand the image one earns by boldly proclaiming their desire to have wealth. Perhaps this is partially a consequence of a value system that rates a comfortable lifestyle as a necessity, thereby defining money as a means to an end rather than an end in itself.

Table 5.1
How Many Adults Consider Each of These Elements to be Very Important in Their Life?

element of life	all adults	Busters
family	96%	93%
health	90	84
your time	79	78
your friends	76	64
religion	69	54
the Bible	67	56
your free time	64	52
living comfortably	60	61
your career	54	67
your community	52	28
money	40	40
government and politics	34	26

Source: Barna Research Group, Ltd.

Ever the pragmatic group, Busters tend to view personal investment in community affairs and in politics and government as being of minimal importance. Given a choice of devoting resources to pursuits that will result in personal gain or in pursuits that will benefit mankind in general, the former option will get the nod every time. Only one-quarter of the Busters described their community or government and politics as very important cornerstones of their world view.

In the process of determining their values system, Busters have kept a keen eye on the Boomers. In general, if Boomers are enthralled with something, Busters are immediately suspect of that element. Many Busters seem driven by one chief value: to avoid embracing the same perspectives and values as the Boomers. Concurrently, however, Busters are struggling to create a more pleasing and acceptable alternative system.

Skepticism Revealed

Like the rest of our society, Busters exhibit a growing disenchantment with institutions. There are few organizations or institutions in which a majority of Busters believe they can place a lot of confidence. What makes their lack of trust in institutions so significant is the fact that Busters, more than older generations, have had little interaction with, and apparently have less knowledge about, most of these institutions.

The entities of which Busters are most trusting are the military and hospitals or health care organizations. These were the only two types of institutions in which a majority of Busters said they had a lot of confidence. Amazingly, they were much

How Many Adults Consider Each of These Elements to be Very Important in Their Life?

Busters
All adults

family 96% 93%
religion 69% 54%
the Bible 67% 56%
money 40% 40%
your community 52% 28%

Source: Barna Research Group, Ltd.

more likely than older adults to assert such a level of trust in the health-related organizations.

Non-profit organizations filled the next echelon on the confidence scale. Christian churches were assigned a lot of confidence by 44%; charities and non-profit organizations, in general, by 36% of the young adults; and the public schools by 32%. The other entity which made this level was the Supreme Court, in which 34% said they had a lot of confidence.

Filling the lower end of the scale were Congress (21%), private business (21%), and the media (13%).

Overall, these levels of confidence suggest that Busters do not differ radically from their elders when it comes to having both low and shrinking levels of confidence in major institutions. The statistics further indicate that the more contact Busters have with a given type of organization, the less confidence they are likely to have in that entity.

Table 5.2
The Percentage of Adults Who Have a Lot of Confidence in Major Institutions

institution	all adults	Busters
the military	58%	59%
hospitals, health care	40	51
Christian churches	43	44
charities, non-profits	23	36
Supreme Court	28	34
the public schools	27	32
private business	20	21
Congress	16	21
the media	10	13

Source: Barna Research Group, Ltd.

Politically Correct, Emotionally Uncertain

Perhaps it is not surprising that the first true philosophical movement to take root during the Busters' years on the college campus is the so-called "politically correct" movement. This, of course, has been the activity taking place at colleges and universities nationwide in which a hyper-sensitivity to language, behavior and thought related to sexual, racial and political realities leaps to center stage of every discussion and decision.

The PC movement has been described by some as Nineties equivalent of radical ideology in the Sixties; by others as a new form of censorship imposed by the Left; and by others as the inevitable quest of thinking people to become loving and sensitive to others regardless of heritage, standing or other false definitions of being. The reality of the core of the PC movement greatly depends upon one's view of the validity of the movement's ideological base.

It is hardly coincidental that the movement sprang to the surface just as Busters have been filling college classrooms. Not since the mid-Sixties has there been a group of students so committed to exploring alternative ex-

The Percentage of Adults Who Have a Lot of Confidence in Major Institutions

Busters
All adults

	hospitals, health care	charities, non-profits	the public schools	Congress	the media
All adults	40%	23%	27%	16%	10%
Busters	51%	36%	32%	21%	13%

Source: Barna Research Group, Ltd.

pressions of reality toward arriving at a new, more palatable and more efficient value system. Much of what the PC proponents push gels with the basic direction in which most Busters are heading in the values quest: equality, justice, freedom, truth, opportunity, love, individualism within a community framework, etc. Calls to action on behalf of the movement have found many young people willing to take up the mantle of the movement in the hope that, at last, this may be what they have been searching for.

> **"Not since the mid-Sixties has there been a group of students so committed to exploring alternative expressions of reality toward arriving at a new, more palatable and more efficient value system."**

The more important circumstance, though, is that the politically correct dogma has found few long-term zealots among Busters. As they have with other philosophies, they have dabbled in it and culled those few elements which they have deemed viable. For the most part, they appreciate the PC approach for calling attention to key issues and for promoting an alternative response to mainstream ideas.

However, this generation has not bought into PC as their answer. Unlike the Boomers, who were often persuaded by seductive rhetoric or magnetic emotional charms, the Busters are not seeking a veneer but a vision with depth. They have lived through the quick-fix society; ironically, it will be they, not their parents, who will ultimately pay the lion's share of the price for that addiction to immediate response.

This is not to suggest that the spin doctors of PC-ism have squandered their time preaching the benefits of multicultural sensitivity. The politically correct philosophy has undeniably caused the Busters to look at some very serious matters through a new lens. The PC perspective has even caused them to alter their positions on some issues in minor ways. But the Busters have not—and, it appears, will not—be forever aligned with or even swayed by the politically correct approach to morality and values.

Weaving the Threads Together

Busters, like most Americans, do not live by a coherent philosophy of life. While about half of the Busters (49%) claim they have an articulated world view, or philosophy, the substance of that world view comes across as superficial in many cases. "Live and let live" or "you have to believe in yourself; just never give up" are representative of the breadth and depth of the driving perspective described by some Busters as their philosophy of life.

Despite the failure of most Busters to develop a significant world view, most of them do possess attitudes and opinions on critical topics. The sum of these views may well represent the psychological filter through which they make their daily decisions. Comprehending these views further clarifies the heart of the Buster generation.

As you examine the data provided in Tables 5.3 and 5.4, keep in mind that a majority of Busters displayed intense feelings about just four of the three dozen perspectives studied. This is crucial to understanding the emotional and intellectual torment in which the Busters currently are enmeshed. Their struggle to make sense of the world and to create a rational plan for their future is mitigated by their inability thus far to grasp views which they hold intensely and which will consequently shape their beliefs and behavior. Chances are good that until this generation can identify those issues which serve as their boundaries or energizers—i.e. the elements worth fighting for—they will wander through life in a confusing and frustrating search for significance and satisfaction.

Views on Behavior and Morality

Busters have some strong feelings when it comes to moral behavior. In fact, of the four items mentioned for which a majority of Busters had intense feelings, three of those related to morality.

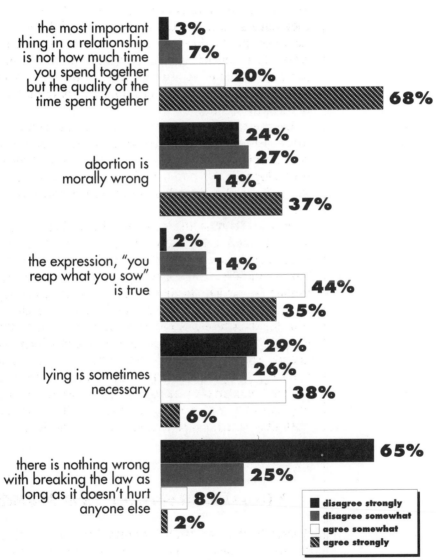

Busters' Views on Matters of Morality and Behavior

the most important thing in a relationship is not how much time you spend together but the quality of the time spent together
- 3%
- 7%
- 20%
- 68%

abortion is morally wrong
- 24%
- 27%
- 14%
- 37%

the expression, "you reap what you sow" is true
- 2%
- 14%
- 44%
- 35%

lying is sometimes necessary
- 29%
- 26%
- 38%
- 6%

there is nothing wrong with breaking the law as long as it doesn't hurt anyone else
- 65%
- 25%
- 8%
- 2%

■ disagree strongly
■ disagree somewhat
□ agree somewhat
▨ agree strongly

Note: Due to rounding and some respondents who did not have an opinion, some figures do not add up to 100%
Source: Barna Research Group, Ltd.

Generally speaking, Busters view the law as rules which should be followed, regardless of the actual effect upon those who might be impacted by the breaking of a law. Two-thirds of the Busters strongly disagreed that there is nothing wrong with breaking a law as long as nobody is harmed in the process. Along a similar vein, a majority of young adults strongly disagreed that "it is better to get even than to get mad." Note that both of these approaches to life receive stronger support from Boomers than Busters, attesting to the Boomers' proclivity to reject those rules not to their liking. Busters are more likely to accept and work within the system.

Busters, like other generations, have embraced the notion of quality time as an acceptable substitute for quantity time in their relationships. Two-thirds of the segment believe that the quality of time spent together is more important than the amount of time committed to the development of a relationship. This may help to explain the frustration so many Busters experience in the pursuit of lasting and meaningful friendships. Yet, this perspective is one of the legacies of the Boomer generation—a legacy that does not serve the inheritors well.

"To the typical Buster, there is no such thing as absolute truth. Statistically, 70% claim that absolute truth does not exist, that all truth is relative and personal."

Busters also struggle with certain aspects of morality. On the one hand, most of them believe that you reap what you sow. On the other hand, when it comes down to specific issues, the lines become more fuzzy for them, in all areas of life.

For instance, Busters are evenly divided on the matter of abortion. Half feel it is morally wrong, half view it as morally acceptable. What makes this more intriguing is the fact that about two-thirds of the Busters say that while they (or their partner) would not have an abortion, it ought to be permitted for others. In discussing abortion as a matter of law, therefore, many Busters would ignore their views on the morality of the matter, apparently deciding that their personal moral views ought not to impact the determination of law.

There is somewhat greater clarity regarding the possibility of intentionally deceiving people. A majority of Busters disagree that lying is sometimes necessary. However, a sizable contingent (44%) assert that sometimes it is "necessary." This perception coincides with the widespread acceptance of relative truth among the Busters: you do what you have to, regardless of the implications or inconsistency of such behavior with your overriding perspectives on life.

To the typical Buster, there is no such thing as absolute truth. Statistically, 70% claim that absolute truth does not exist, that all truth is relative and personal. This view is supported by their belief that everything in life is negotiable. In this way of viewing the world, since there are no absolutes, all decisions and realities can be debated until an accommodation is reached between the parties involved.

This type of experiential, negotiated reality is made possible by the notion that you cannot trust anything of which you do not personally have a first-hand knowledge or experience. Two-thirds of the Buster generation concede that "nothing can be known for certain except the things that you experience in your own life." Burned by people and organizations in the past, and trained by their parents to be wary of a deceitful world, Busters have matured into world-class skeptics and generally do not take claims about reality at face value. Busters believe what they can feel, taste, see, hear and touch—and very little else.

Meaning and Goals

From the Buster vantage point, it is important to know what you are about and to devote yourself to protecting what you have.

Two-thirds of the young generation confirm that "if you don't look out for your own best interests, you can be sure no one else will either." Yet, they also believe that people are basically good. How do they reconcile these seemingly contradictory statements?

Simply, they contend that it's a competitive world; you have to do what you have to do to get by these days. Ultimately, a person's first and foremost responsibility is to himself or herself. Agonizing over world problems and societal ills is laudable, perhaps, but impractical in this day and age. For instance, Busters reject a notion popular among older adults that poverty is a consequence of laziness. Not so, say the Busters. You can work your tail off and have little to show for the effort because life is not fair and the struggle to reach the comfort zone is getting tougher every day.

Table 5.3
Busters' Views on Matters of Morality and Behavior

statement	——agree——		——disagree——	
	strongly	somewhat	somewhat	strongly
• there is nothing wrong with breaking the law as long as it doesn't hurt anyone else	2%	8%	25%	65%
• lying is sometimes necessary	6	38	26	29
• it is better to get even than to get mad	13	9	20	57
• the expression "you reap what you sow" is true	35	44	14	2
• abortion is morally wrong	37	14	27	24
• the most important thing in a relationship is not how much time you spend together but the quality of the time spent together	68	20	7	3

Source: Barna Research Group, Ltd.

Table 5.4
Busters' Views on Purpose and Satisfaction in Life

statement	agree		disagree	
	strongly	somewhat	somewhat	strongly
• one person can really make a difference in the world these days	33%	42%	18%	7%
• the purpose of life is enjoyment and personal fulfillment	32	33	22	11
• if you don't look out for your own best interests, you can be sure that no one else will either	30	34	22	15
• people are basically good	29	53	9	8
• your first responsibility is to yourself	29	27	19	25
• no matter how you feel about money, it is still the main symbol of success in life	19	30	25	26
• you can usually tell how successful a person is by examining what they own	10	16	19	54
• most poor people are poor because they're lazy	5	18	34	43

Source: Barna Research Group, Ltd.

In the end, Busters generally concur that the struggle is worth it if you can achieve meaning in life. To the Buster mind, how is that defined? Two-thirds of them describe the purpose of life as enjoyment and personal fulfillment. And probably the dominant avenue to reaching such joy is through the accumulation of sufficient wealth to acquire that which brings pleasure and comfort. About half of the Busters say that money remains the primary symbol of success, certainly a viable means to realizing the levels of fun and fulfillment that make getting up each morning a worthwhile endeavor.

Busters are young but not wholly naive about the prospects for success in our culture. Most of them admit that life is no simple process. Yet, the majority insist that any individual can achieve great things. Three-quarters of the Busters still believe—in spite of their diminished interest in fighting for causes, in spite of their anger toward the convoluted world they're inheriting from the Boomers, and in spite of their jaded perspective on the world—that one person can make a difference in the world these days. Busters will admit that money is not the only way of measuring a person's success, but it represents one of the more visible and secure means to reaching one's goals in life.

Sources of Influence

Busters are certainly aware that the media have an influence on their thinking. What is surprising, though, is how accepting they seem to be of the influence of the media.

Without a doubt, the typical Buster believes that the world is out of control these days. They know this based upon personal experience (the only truly credible source for a Buster), confirmed by the mass media.

The power of that confirmation by the media is not to be minimized. Did you realize that *nearly thirty million Busters believe that the values and lifestyles shown in movies, television programs, and music videos are an **accurate, representative** depiction of the way that Americans think and live these days?* While this represents a minority view, it is a substantial number of people nevertheless.

Further, in assessing the news media, Busters are equally likely to characterize journalists as "fair and objective in their reporting of the news" as they are to ascribe significant levels of bias in their reporting.

It is likely that Busters, like the rest of us, have no real sense of where reality starts and where the media (or any other source of influence) take over and reshape our perceptions of reality. But it also seems clear that more than any prior generation, the Busters have embraced television, in particular, as a credible creator of those perceptions. Raised on the tube, they now accept it as another member of the family, an electronic sibling imparting both wisdom and entertainment as desired. In an odd way, Busters appear to assign greater credibility to the medium than to the people who program that medium. What a tribute to the power of technology!

Contours of the Heart

These myriad influences and perspectives, then, are blended into a complex package that shapes the heart and soul of the Buster. What is the end result?

Let me propose a ten-point description of the prevailing view of the Buster, a profile of the character of the heart of this generation based upon their values, morals, ethical considerations, and core perspectives.

Busters Are Disillusioned

More than any prior generation, they feel estranged from God, separated from each other, lacking meaning in life, void of roots and a societal connection. In short, they feel alienated from life. They are skeptical because they have experienced deception and rampant superficiality. Their skepticism, though, is not a sophisticated cynicism so much as a defense mechanism hiding a raw helplessness over their circumstances in life. They lack heroes, causes, vision, and sadly, an abiding hope in the goodness of their future.

Busters Feel Abandoned

America has been called the home of the brave, but it has more commonly served as a safe nesting place for weary and wounded. No more. Busters believe they are getting a raw deal. They are being cheated not only out of the wealth that would traditionally have been theirs, but are also losing out on the other resources and commitments that could have been left in place to assure them a nurturing and worthwhile existence. They expect to raise their own families differently as a result of what they have experienced, but in the meantime they resent having been forgotten by their parents and the older generations.

Busters Desire a High Quality of Life

This is not a generation anxious to settle for whatever is left over. They want it all, they want it now, and they are not content to hear excuses from the Boomers as to why they cannot reasonably expect it. The fact that they are unlikely to exceed the standards for quality of life set by their parents has created a smoldering anger and resentment in them. Quality of life, for them, dictates a high "fun" quotient, sans sacrifice.

Busters Are Independent

They have been raised to think and act according to their instincts. They behave as individuals, unfettered by corporate ties to family or organization. They may listen to counsel, but they make their own decisions and generally reject demands handed down without debate.

Busters Are Defensive

Bred in an age of materialism and prosperity, they expected more than they are apparently going to receive. Consequently, they are protective of what they possess and determined to achieve whatever is possible. They have learned that people may mean well, but they generally cannot be trusted since it's every man for himself in a competitive world.

Busters Are Comfortable with Change

They grew up in the midst of chaos; they know nothing else. They are used to the fast pace and the lack of stability. Traditions are short-lived for Busters. They are more interested in doing what will work than what honors the past or provides emotional security. Taken from another perspective, realize that they actively embrace change because it enables them to reject the Boomer mindset and culture.

Busters Are More Sensitive to People

Boomers were driven by their objectives, which often meant crushing others in their charge to the top. Busters, while desirous of good salaries and substantial influences, are less career-driven, less impersonal about life. They are returning to a more conventional desire to build lasting relationships and to exhibit sensitivity to people. Although the trust factor is absent, they maintain a strong desire to reach their goals by building in cooperation with others who have common interests. They do not commit easily or quickly, but their commitments are more meaningful than those of the Boomers.

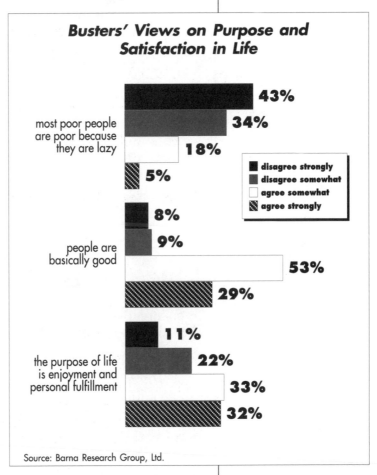

Busters' Views on Purpose and Satisfaction in Life

most poor people are poor because they are lazy
- 43%
- 34%
- 18%
- 5%

■ disagree strongly
■ disagree somewhat
□ agree somewhat
▨ agree strongly

people are basically good
- 8%
- 9%
- 53%
- 29%

the purpose of life is enjoyment and personal fulfillment
- 11%
- 22%
- 33%
- 32%

Source: Barna Research Group, Ltd.

Busters Are Pluralists

They have no problem accepting competing points of view, or allowing seemingly contradictory perspectives or efforts to co-exist. Whether it is religion, politics, relationships, or other areas of endeavor, expect Busters to be accepting of divergent approaches.

Busters Are Flexible

There are few absolutes and few immovable standards in their lives. They maintain a fluidity to life that facilitates rapid change, addressing unforeseen opportunities, exploration of unique strategies, and the like. They are persuaded by what works, not what "ought" to be.

Busters are Pragmatic

Don't waste time by explaining theory to a Buster. They want to get on with life, exploiting the practical. Lacking a holistic sense of mission or a comprehensive world view, they cope on a situational basis. Denying the existence of absolute truths, they handle each situation on its own apparent merit and potential, responding as best they can given the available inputs.

What It Looks Like

In practice, then, dealing with Busters may be a novel experience for you. If you're used to handling the needs and concerns of older adults, hold on for some challenges.

For example, the typical Buster puts no stock in a chain of command. They will not so much attack the hierarchy as ignore it. They'll seek to incorporate their own thinking and energies into the process. If their contribution is not appreciated, they'll work around the process or go elsewhere.

Don't expect Busters to over-exert themselves. Their view of the world is one of an eye for an eye. They are contract players, hired for a specific exchange of commensurately valued realities. They do not believe in paying their dues; if you want them to put out, you'll have to pay them off at the same time. Encounters in life are, to Busters, simple trade-offs in real time.

There are no sacrifices made today for possible gain in the future. Buster life is a real time, zero sum game.

They take this seriously, by the way. America has never experienced a suicide rate as high among any previous generation. More than five thousand Busters commit suicide each year. The suicide rate has more than doubled since Boomers were in their teens and early twenties. Ever the pragmatic group, Busters calculate the risks and the payoffs and act. If the future unfolds in as bleak a manner as many of them anticipate, suicide will be just one of the severe outcomes of their shattered dreams.

BEHIND *The Facade*

Natalie Bazajarian ◆ Age: 18

"If that kid asks me 'why' one more time, I'm gonna go berserk."
Managing the Buster can be a challenge. Just ask Stan Wieslowski.

"Natalie is a good kid. She gets to work on time; she usually shows up for her shift; she doesn't cause personnel problems. But, geez! Every decision we make is challenged! She always wants to know why we made that choice. And she's not the only one. Most of our young employees have the same style. It can get very tiring, always explaining yourself and your motives."

Why keep her on?

"Oh, don't get me wrong," the manager hastily apologizes. *"Natalie has some real strengths. She's pretty good about changing tasks quickly. She is good with the computer. And she seems pretty self-motivated, as long as it's normal working hours. No, overall, she's okay."*

The independent streak of Busters can be a real challenge for managers like Stan. While the Natalies of the Buster generation are common, understanding them is not. It

> **"Every decision we make is challenged! She always wants to know why we made that choice. And she's not the only one. Most of our young employees have the same style."**

took Stan several months before he came to grips with her personality and capabilities.

"Natalie wants to know how it all fits together before she'll put herself into the job. Now for an executive, I can see that. But a part-time kid making $6 an hour? Unreal."

Stan pauses and shakes his head.

"Young people today don't swallow the party line. They hear the instructions, but they want to know the motivations and the rationale behind the instructions. I've got two choices, really. I can deal with their constant questioning and hope that they buy into what we're about, or I can refuse to respond and tell them to just do the job. I tried that approach at first. They all left within a week or two of realizing that they wouldn't get their answers. So, if I want young folks to play a role in our company, even a minor role, I think this is part of the price I have to pay. Hey, it's cheaper than a raise," he summarizes with a chuckle.

Six

By Their Deeds You Will Know Them

EMEMBER THE OLD ADMONITION, "DO AS I SAY, NOT AS I do"?

The impetus behind that comment was that the true nature of the individual is most evident by examining how they behave, regardless of what they say or teach. Indeed, the recent experiences of political leaders such as Gary Hart, Joseph Biden, and Ted Kennedy demonstrate the importance of people's actions. These men were rejected by voters not so much because of their political stands but because of the message sent by their behavior. In the same manner, it is instructive to observe the ways in which Baby Busters live.

We can derive a more complete understanding of the Busters by exploring how they spend their time, their relationship with the media and entertainment vehicles, their involvement with societal needs and causes, their response to economic hardships, and their health.

Using a Precious Resource

For decades, money reigned as the most precious resource, but Baby Boomers made time the issue. Boomers jealousy guarded their time; they made the allocation of their waking hours the ultimate yardstick of the value they attached to any activity, relationship, product, or endeavor.

Busters, while treasuring their time—especially their leisure time—are not nearly as psychotic about time as were (and, in most cases, are) their parents. Nevertheless, they devote themselves to the wide range of available activities with great care.

Consider some of the activities they might engage in during a typical week.

> ➤ More than 95% of them watch television during the week. The typical Buster devotes more than three hours each day to viewing programming. They, are attracted to cable stations, which tend to focus on more specialized types of programming, addressing some of the unique interests of the Buster generation. MTV, of course, is the prime example of such niche-based programming. In a typical week, four out of ten Busters (38%) view MTV, making it one of the most widely viewed television networks among Busters, and making Busters the dominant audience of that music channel.

> ➤ Almost four out of ten Busters engage in religious activities during a week. About 36% attend a religious service in a typical week; one-third reads from the Bible, outside of a church; and 15% will attend a Sunday school class at a church. While there is a significant religious rethinking taking place among the Busters, many continue to patronize the same religious institutions in which they were raised.

➤ While more than nine out of ten Busters watch television and about eight out of ten listen to the radio in a typical day, reading continues to have a widespread, albeit declining following. Seven out of ten Busters (71%) read part of a book, other than the Bible, during a typical week. Busters are reading somewhat fewer books per year than did prior generations, and they are shifting the type of reading in which they engage.

➤ Physical fitness remains important to Busters, accounting for the fact that two-thirds of the segment participate in exercise or athletic activities in a given week. More of the athletic activity of Busters is solo than team activity, a response to the fragmented schedules of today's population. Fewer Busters are involved in basketball, football, soccer, baseball and ice hockey—the traditional team sports—than was true in the past. Larger numbers of Busters are active in one-person and two-person sports such as tennis, bowling, swimming, bicycling, running/jogging, and racquetball.

➤ About one-quarter of the Busters volunteer their time in a given week to help some type of non-profit organization or church. This work is apparently on the decline among Busters, as they often find that they can discern no direct payback or impact in response to their efforts.

If we change the focus of our attention from weekly activities to the activities in which Busters engage during a typical month, we find that similar trends surface. Among those are:

➤ a majority of Busters have some formal engagement with religious organizations;

➤ one-third actively pursue information through the electronic or print media related to religious instruction and perspectives;

➤ four out of ten discuss their religious beliefs with others whom they believe maintain different religious views;

Table 6.1

Activities in Which Busters Have Participated in the Last 30 Days

activity	participation
• went to a theatre to watch a movie	78%
• participated in corporate religion	55
• were exposed to religious radio or television	44
• volunteered time to help needy people in their area	44
• discussed religious beliefs with someone of different beliefs	42
• read a religious publication or book, other than the Bible	31
• attended a class at a school or training center	30
• volunteered time to help a non-profit organization or a church	27
• avoided buying a specific product or brand because it was being boycotted by a cause or organization they support	21
• volunteered time to help needy people in other countries	17

Source: Barna Research Group, Ltd.

➤ nearly half volunteer their time to help needy people in their area. Critically important, though, is the realization that much of the volunteerism happens apart from organization-driven efforts; that is, Busters will lend a hand to the needy on their own, or in conjunction with friends and family who share the desire to make a difference. Also note that Busters are much more likely to engage in volunteer activity that aids domestic causes than that aimed at minimizing international problems;

➤ one-fifth support boycotts of products, services, and companies by changing their buying patterns to reject the items offered by the organizations being boycotted;

➤ three out of ten Busters are currently enrolled in a formal education program;

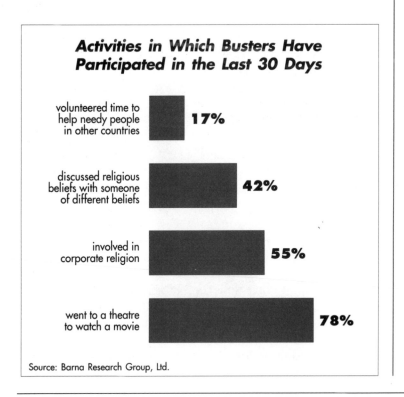

Activities in Which Busters Have Participated in the Last 30 Days

volunteered time to help needy people in other countries	17%
discussed religious beliefs with someone of different beliefs	42%
involved in corporate religion	55%
went to a theatre to watch a movie	78%

Source: Barna Research Group, Ltd.

> ➤ eight out of ten go to the movie theatre each month to be entertained;

> ➤ and only a small percentage of Busters (26%) donate money to non-profit organizations other than churches.

Table 6.2

How Busters Are Spending Their Time Compared to One Year Ago

activity	time devoted now, compared to last year		
	more	same	less
• working at your job	53%	26%	20%
• seeking additional formal education	46	23	29
• being at home with family	43	29	27
• exercising, working out physically	42	28	31
• reading for pleasure	41	21	37
• being with friends	40	25	35
• volunteering	24	34	41
• watching television	19	28	52
• participating in church or a place of religious involvement	17	35	46

Source: Barna Research Group, Ltd.

Further insight is drawn from an examination of how Busters are reshaping their time commitments. In comparing how they spent their time a year earlier with how they presently commit their time, the statistics show that the net increases in time commitments are being given to being at home with family; exercising or engaging in physical workouts; and seeking formal education.

The largest increase of all, though, is associated with employment. Only a portion of this increase can be attributed to the numbers of Busters who are entering the job market for the first time. Most of those who are expanding their work week have been in the job market for a few years and are now beginning to accelerate their time commitment to their careers, in spite of the fact that most of those individuals are neither career-driven nor expect to stay with their employer for prolonged periods of time. The conflict between attitudes toward job and the effort expended in the work place will be addressed in the succeeding chapter.

Also recognize some of the activities on which a growing proportion of Busters are spending less time. The biggest losers are television viewing, participation in organized religion, and volunteerism. There has been little change in the aggregate numbers of Busters who are involved in reading for pleasure or who are spending time with friends.

Media and Entertainment

The role of technology and electronics in the lives of Busters is central. They are more than simply the generation that was raised by television. They are a generation whose response to their world is both stimulated by and transmitted through various technological impulses.

Numerous studies have been conducted, and books written about, the enormous influence of television on the minds of today's young adults. Apart from the impact of the tube on their values and behavior, what remains fascinating is their loyalty to the TV set. Only 4% of the Busters describe the content of current television programming to be excellent. Almost two-thirds (64%) rate network programming as fair, not too good, or poor. Yet, they continue to watch and continue to believe the information that is broadcast.

Perhaps most incredible is the fact that Busters are the first generation of which a majority states that they actually like commercials. Busters view commercials as a means of remaining abreast of trends in communication skills, fashion, music and emotional response. They believe that all products ought to be allowed to advertise (67%). And nearly three-quarters of the Busters contend that the quality of advertising is improving.

More than nine out of ten Busters own a television set and about two-thirds subscribe to cable television. An important feature of the TV for Busters is the VCR; two-thirds (67%) of them currently own a VCR. Almost all of these VCR owners indicate that during the course of a typical month they either buy or rent video pre-recorded cassettes (PRCs). Busters are not accustomed to taping programs for future playback; they are more likely than most adults to live in "real time:" if they miss and event, they miss it.

Nearly every Buster who owns a VCR rents or buys movies for their viewing pleasure. While Builders and Seniors grew up thinking of movies as a special attraction, and Boomers treated movies like a reward for good behavior, Busters have integrated movies into their life routine no differently than their seniors have incorporated radios into their courses of activity.

Above all else, Busters love to be entertained. This passion for high-gloss, big-screen entertainment is confirmed by the movie studios, who unabashedly admit that they develop most of their movies with the Buster audience in mind. People under the age of 25 account for more than half of the $5 billion of revenues generated by movie theatres today. And they are responsible for several billion dollars more in revenues generated by the sale and rental of PRCs.

Besides movies, the most popular PRCs are those featuring sports events (rented or purchased during the past 12 months by 27% of the Busters who own a VCR) and musical concerts or performances (26%). Notice that both of these categories of PRC feature entertainment—the magnet that attracts Busters. Less commonly acquired PRCs feature exercise or fitness routines (rented or purchased by 17% in the past year) and Christian teaching or entertainment (13%, mostly related to the entertainment offerings). Instructional videos and other types of videos are slow movers with this audience.

In focusing upon sales figures or technology, it is easy to overlook a crucial insight represented by the video preferences of Busters. Video stimuli are critical to reaching the Buster population. Weaned on *Sesame Street*, a blizzard of 30-second and 15-second commercials, and (later) MTV and its imitators, Busters respond dramatically to video presentations—at home, in the workplace, at school, and even in churches. The newer computer technologies which provide interactive graphics (such as CD-ROM systems and other software featuring graphics continuity) also find a special place in the Buster market.

The significance of video has even impacted Busters' response to printed materials. They are more drawn to bright colors, short copy, pictures, and connotations of fun and movement than were previous generations. While advertising and communications have always struggled to capture people's attention by grabbing the eye and intriguing the mind, successfully attracting Busters has become a more difficult adventure.

Other technologies, besides the television

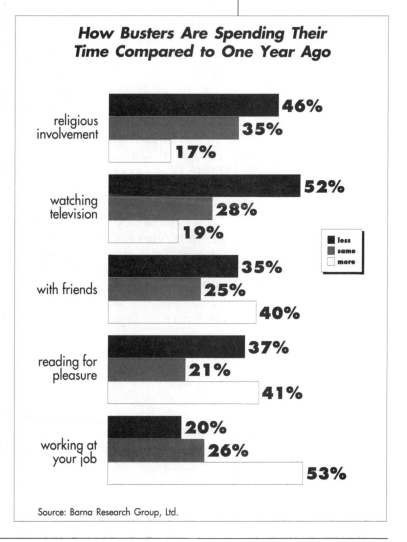

How Busters Are Spending Their Time Compared to One Year Ago

religious involvement — 46%, 35%, 17%

watching television — 52%, 28%, 19%

less / same / more

with friends — 35%, 25%, 40%

reading for pleasure — 37%, 21%, 41%

working at your job — 20%, 26%, 53%

Source: Barna Research Group, Ltd.

and its VCR sidekick, have captured the fancy of the emerging generation. A prime example is the personal computer. Unknown just ten years ago, PCs have rapidly become common to most Busters. Relatively few are gripped by the PC-fear that has limited or even paralyzed so many older adults who are seeking to remain competitive in the marketplace.

Three out of every ten Busters own a personal computer at home. The fact that this is a higher proportion than exists among older adults is astounding given both the limited discretionary incomes of Busters and their moderate job status and consequent need for such technology outside the place of employment.

Music being the critical lifestyle element that it is—Busters outspend all other population segments combined on concerts and recorded music—you may not be surprised to discover that Busters are also the most prolific buyers of compact disc players. Almost half of the Busters 18 or older already own a CD player. That's about 50% higher than the proportion of Boomers who own such equipment.

The other essential pieces of electronic equipment for Busters are the stereo unit (owned by an overwhelming majority) and a telephone answering machine (in place for 57% of the Busters). Less commonly owned electronics include a cellular car phone (about 7%), a home fax machine (4%) and a satellite dish for television reception (6%).

Literacy Is Not Dead. Yet.

Undeniably, literacy levels in America are on the decline. There are various reasons for this. The demise of public school education, the influx of functionally (and culturally) illiterate immigrants, and the profound influence of television and videos on the training and imaginations of our young people are all significant contributors to the condition.

Nevertheless, a majority of Busters purchased books within the past 12 months (60%). While this is not as widespread as among older population segments, neither does it suggest a

Two Generations, Two Perspectives

A **Subjective** View of How Boomers and Busters Evaluate Their World

	Busters	Boomers
ARSENIO HALL	sensitive; hip; politically correct; relational	is he literate?! needs a haircut; poor interviewer
RED HOT CHILI PEPPERS	on the edge; good message; pioneering sound; music with an attitude	over the edge; best tattoos since Johnny Winter; anger without a cause
WAYNE'S WORLD	hilarious farce; good music; worthy message	cheap remake of Bill and Ted; good music; no message; too amateurish
THE SIMPSONS	sharp cultural insights; very current; just like my family	gets old quick; Bart needs a lickin'; trite commentary
HOWARD STERN	irrelevant; ill-mannered; sophomoric; get a *real* job	courageous; underscores cultural prudishness; social critic; funny
MTV SPORTS	hip; global; adventurous; great balance of music, video, & sport	pure fluff; these are not *real* sports; hire a professional cameraman
NEIL SIMON	who? contrived; repetitious; too slick	clever writing; deep human insights
SATURDAY NIGHT LIVE	takes risks; eclectic; good ensemble; beats prime-time programming	not what it used to be; on too late; you call this music?

generation that is wholly distanced from books. In fairness, realize that not only is the number of young adults who read for pleasure and who buy books during the year on the decline, but also declining are the number of books purchased per person and the amounts of time spent reading by those who do read for pleasure.

What kind of books do Busters buy? By far the most popular types of books are fictional novels (acquired by 67% of the Busters last year). No other genre of literature was bought by at least half of the 18-or-older Busters during the prior 12 months. Other types of books that were popular were business-related books (purchased by 45%); children's books (33%); biographies (32%); self-help and self-improvement books (27%); and Christian books, other than the Bible (18%).

The ranking of these categories fits the Buster mentality like a glove. What sells best? Entertainment. What trails most closely? The most pragmatic of subject areas, business and career-related books. What is the largest niche market within the Buster segment? Children's books, for those young adults who are starting their family and wish to spend quality time interacting with their children.

Taking a Stand, Getting Involved

Busters have earned a reputation within the mass media as the activist generation. Their efforts to raise attention in relation to the environment, homelessness, and similar national and international difficulties have led many to think of Busters as cause-driven zealots.

While Busters do get involved in shaping their world, depicting them as an activist generation is an inaccurate portrayal. Consider the realities of their societal involvement.

➤ They are less likely than other adults to write to elected officials to express their opinion on current issues.

➤ One-fifth of the Busters may be involved in boycotts of products, brands or companies in a given month. This, too, is equal to or lower than the participation rates of older adults.

➤ Busters are the least likely to identify a cause for which they would be willing to die.

➤ Of all adult age groups, Busters have the lowest proportion registered to vote. Even among registered voters, their turnout at the polls on election day has been the lowest for each of the last three national elections (1988 to 1992), when Busters first became eligible to vote.

➤ Busters are less likely to donate money to causes or charities than were prior generations at a similar stage in their life cycle.

➤ While millions of Busters sacrifice their time to work as volunteers at churches and other non-profit organizations, they are less willing to do so than are older adults. Studies indicate that they are not expecting to increase their volunteer time in the near future.

Interestingly, one of our recent studies explored the likelihood of Busters boycotting the products of advertisers who promote their products on television programs which have substantially above-average levels of violence, sexual activity, profanity, or liberal values.

Most Busters concur that the concept of boycotts is viable: 73% disagreed with a statement that "participating in boycotts of products or companies does not really accomplish anything." Yet, most Busters are not committed enough to change through this forum to engage in such activity.

Half of the Busters believe that network television programming currently has too much violence; just 17% said they were very likely to boycott the advertisers supporting those shows.

(Meanwhile 29% of older adults said they would be willing to boycott such advertisers.)

Sexual activity in network programs was deemed too high by 36% of the Busters; 23% of these young adults said they would be very likely to boycott those advertisers (versus 31% of older adults).

Three out of ten Busters stated that network shows contain excessive profanity; 15% said they might boycott as a result.

One-third of the Busters were troubled by the excessive demonstration of "non-traditional or liberal values" broadcast by the networks; 20% said this would motivate them to boycott (23% of their elders concurred).

All Is Not Well

Government statistics provide yet another slant on the lifestyle realities for Busters. They do spend less money on health care than older adults and make fewer visits to a physician during a typical year. The typical Buster visits doctors four times a year; Boomers, five times; Builders, six times; Seniors, nine times.

But these numbers mask another stark reality: Busters may be the unhealthiest generation of young adults we have witnessed in many decades. On a per capita basis, Busters have a much higher incidence of infections and parasites, respiratory ailments, digestive tract problems, and minor injuries than do older adults. The genesis of these difficulties is hard to pinpoint, but includes less nutritional dietary habits, sexual promiscuity, frequent foreign travel, and general ignorance about health care.

The encouraging sign is that those activities which Busters clearly recognize to be pernicious—such as drug abuse, alcohol abuse and smoking—are all on the decline.

Not What You Expected?

Busters represent a very different type of young adult than we have seen in the past.

They were raised on television and while they refuse to ignore its flaws, they refuse to turn it off.

They are conscious of the harsh economic realities they face, and disheartened by the perception that they will probably never rise to the level of financial independence and security achieved by their parents and grandparents. Yet, these realities have failed to curb their upscale tastes, even in light of their mid-scale budgets.

Prior generations couldn't wait to reach the "age of reason" so that they could launch out on their own. Busters, on the other hand, are postponing such unfettered freedom until the last possible moment. Today, nearly six out of ten adults 20 to 24 years of age are still living with their parents. And the average age at which adults get married for the first time continues to rise (it is currently about 25).

Although Busters are relatively sensitive to the importance of protecting the environment, they are also deeply committed to leading a life of fun and frivolity. Much of their fun involves the expending of resources that may harm the environment.

Young adults are typically energetic and adventurous. Today's young adults, though, are more deliberate and intentional in their behavior. Spontaneity, a trademark of youth, is less evident in the lifestyles of Baby Busters than was true for the prior two generations when they were in their early twenties.

Busters have a pensive side and tend to make decisions with a greater focus on long-term outcomes than characterized the Boomers. Yet, when it comes to sex and the spread of AIDS, more than three-quarters of the aggregate Buster segment believes that use of condoms is a superior response to sexual abstinence.

As time goes on, perhaps some of the seeming inconsistencies in the Buster lifestyle will be smoothed out. In the meantime, making hard predictions about their likely activity is tenuous.

BEHIND *The Facade*

Alan Bosworth ◆ Age: 23

Ah, the irony of it all. Alan Bosworth is sipping from his carbonated soda, tapping the side of the aluminum can with his long, bony fingers. A tall, thin young man with longish blond hair, he has on a T-shirt with jeans. The T-shirt has the name of Greenpeace, the environmental protection agency, splashed across the front. Why Greenpeace?

"I don't know, I just thought the concept was very good." It turns out he has never heard of the organization itself. And that fact does not perturb him in the least.

He shares an apartment with two other young men about the same age. Alan works part-time and goes to school part-time. He used to spend large amounts of time volunteering at the regional office of Amnesty International.

"Good people, good cause, good work, but great pizza and parties."

His sense of social consciousness is a consequence of a healthy diet of television viewing. His input comes from Peter Jennings, PBS specials, "The Simpsons," and the interviews he

> **"His input comes from Peter Jennings, PBS specials, 'The Simpsons,' and the interviews he reads occasionally in *Rolling Stone* and *Spin* magazines."**

reads occasionally in *Rolling Stone* and *Spin* magazines. He also gleans insights into his world from the movies he watches on his VCR.

"Spike Lee and John Singleton, they are very hip. Good sense of the streets and what's really happening out there."

Church lost Alan about three years ago.

"Nothing real happening there," he explains. *"When was the last time you visited a church and saw a video clip? Or heard a preacher talk about things that are happening in the streets? It's for another time, another mindset. Sure, I believe in God, but I don't know what churches have to do with knowing God."*

Does he give money to support the causes in which he believes? His answers to such queries are defensive, describing his low wages, his busy schedule, the lack of trust for such non-profit groups, and his desire to research them more carefully before he really gets involved deeply.

"There are lots of good people and good organizations out there, but you have to be careful. Lots of thieves, too. I don't want my money sucked up by the scam artists."

Does his future hold a place for community activism?

"Depends," he says non-committally. *"You can't fight all the fights. You have to pick one or two and really put your energy into it. I haven't found the cause that really does it for me. When I do, yeah, I'll pull my weight."*

Adventures in the Marketplace

THERE WAS A TIME IN AMERICAN HISTORY WHEN GOING TO college was viewed as a privilege because it enhanced people's abilities to comprehend a complex world and increased their potential for leaving a positive mark on that world.

Judging by the experiences and expectations of the Busters, the times have definitely changed. Education remains a desirable commodity in our society, but the reasons for investing in a higher education are now radically different than was the case for the Builders and even for many of the Boomers. As you might expect, the impact of a college degree on a person's career options has also changed in telltale ways.

Sociologists have convincingly demonstrated the tight connection between educational achievement and earnings potential. But the passage of time is loosening the linkage between schooling and income, just as we are less prone these days to associate a college degree with a highly trained, skilled and motivated employee. The reality is that for many Busters, attending college is seen as part of the minimally acceptable route to adulthood. For many employers, a college degree is viewed as a credential of dubious value.

Keeping up with the Joneses

At the turn of the century, attending college was an experience common only to the offspring of the upper class and, perhaps, a few outstanding students from middle class or working class homes. This remained relatively unchanged until the years immediately following the second world war and the Korean War. At that time government funding enabled millions of young men who had fought for their country to have the chance to attend college and earn a degree.

Taking advantage of this boon, young men in the late Forties and throughout the Fifties enrolled in colleges and universities across the land. The prevalent belief was that a college experience was their opportunity to get ahead. Their years in college would afford them the chance to reflect on the issues of life toward arriving at a world view, to have an opportunity to study and assimilate their native culture more fully, and to capture the wisdom of the ages through the exploration of a broad array of disciplines under the guidance of skilled teachers.

Upon graduating and entering the job market, these college educated individuals learned first-hand the impact a degree could have upon their financial fortunes. Consequently, the Builders determined that they would slave and save to ensure that their children (i.e. the Boomers) would have a chance to get a college degree, too.

During the Boomer years college enrollment records were shattered, as millions of these adults pursued their parents' dreams by completing a degree program. In fact, Boomers pushed the boundaries even farther, as millions refused to stop after their initial four years on campus, but went on to pursue a graduate degree. Boomers made graduate degrees nearly as common as Bachelor degrees had been for their grandparents' generation.

Ever the opportunists, Boomers also parlayed their educational achievement into an economic bonanza. Waving their multiple diplomas before employers, they grabbed better paying and higher status positions in major corporations and throughout government, fueling their rise to the financial comfort zone. Based on their positive experience with college training, Boomers certainly believe in the value of a college education and have the lifestyle to support that belief.

But Busters, in general, never witnessed the sacrifice and toil it took for their predecessors to achieve what seems so easily

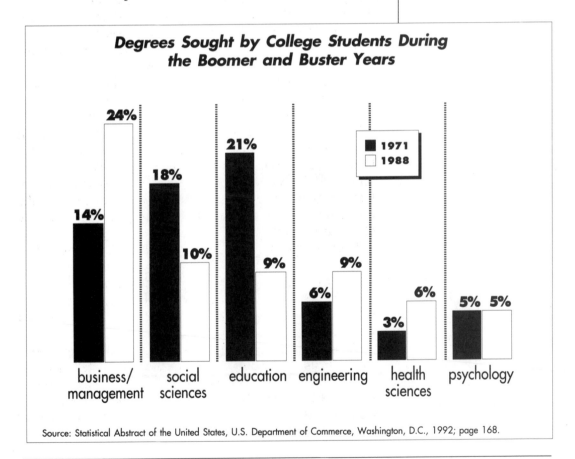

Degrees Sought by College Students During the Boomer and Buster Years

■ 1971
□ 1988

	business/management	social sciences	education	engineering	health sciences	psychology
1971	14%	18%	21%	6%	3%	5%
1988	24%	10%	9%	9%	6%	5%

Source: Statistical Abstract of the United States, U.S. Department of Commerce, Washington, D.C., 1992; page 168.

"These days, Busters attend college because it is the assumed next logical step after high school."

Raised in relative affluence and lacking an understanding of the journey that led to their parents' relative abundance, Busters have a less developed appreciation for the academic life. Given the issues that pulsate with urgency on their life agenda—economic parity, independence, and a sense of purpose—a college degree has limited glitter and appeal to our youngest adults.

Table 7.1

Degrees Sought by College Students During the Boomer and Buster Years

field of study	% of degrees granted, by year	
	1971	1988
business/management	14%	24%
social sciences	18	10
education	21	9
engineering	6	9
health sciences	3	6
communications	1	5
psychology	5	5
computer science	*	4
humanities	8	4
life sciences	4	4
visual/performing arts	4	4

* indicates less than one-half of one percent

Source: Statistical Abstract of the United States, U.S. Department of Commerce, Washington, D.C., 1992; page 168.

These days, Busters attend college because it is the assumed next logical step after high school. They view their time on campus as a job preparation period in which their chief goals are to identify the career they would most enjoy, to acquire the credentials necessary to qualify for the highest paying job, and to establish meaningful marketplace contacts.

The laudable considerations of decades past—acquiring wisdom and intellectual breadth, learning how to reason, refining their cultural sensitivities, developing a philosophy of life—are barely in the scope of the Busters' reflections about college and life after their graduation ceremony. Indeed, Busters would be more likely to view college as a competitive necessity than to see it as a means of becoming a better or more complete human being.

Comparing the college experiences of Boomers and Busters, the data show that Busters are much more likely to seek degrees in the higher paying, high demand, and more practical fields such as business, communications and technology. They are much less likely to pursue degrees in education, the humanities and the social sciences. In fact, the proportion of college students has doubled who are seeking degrees in areas such as law, health sciences and computer science, while the proportion has been cut in half among those seeking degrees in areas such as foreign languages and library science.

Because of the ambivalence of Busters toward obtaining a college degree, increased numbers of this generation initially attend community colleges before transferring to a four-year institution for the completion of their education. Their attitude is not unlike that of a child testing the rolling waters of the ocean: first, stick in the toe, then the whole foot, and if the temperature is satisfactory, plunge in for the full experience.

The data also show that more Busters are dropping out before finishing their studies than was true among Boomers. A related trend is that Busters are taking significantly longer than did the Boomers to complete their studies. It is not uncommon for Busters to take off an extended period of time (i.e. a 12- or 24-month sabbatical) before choosing to go the route. Another popular alternative is to take a lighter course load each term, thereby easing the pressures of the course and prolonging their enrollment period.

Literacy Test Scores: Literature and History

Proportion of Correct Answers on Literature

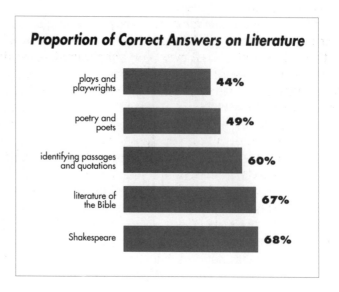

plays and playwrights	44%
poetry and poets	49%
identifying passages and quotations	60%
literature of the Bible	67%
Shakespeare	68%

Proportion of Correct Answers on History

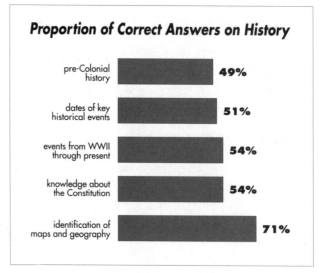

pre-Colonial history	49%
dates of key historical events	51%
events from WWII through present	54%
knowledge about the Constitution	54%
identification of maps and geography	71%

Source: What Do Our 17-Year-Olds Know?, Diane Ravitch and Chester Finn, Jr., Perennial Library, New York, 1988, pages 85-120.

Why are there such different profiles for the Boomers and Busters regarding college education? Much of the distinction is related to their respective views on life. Boomers viewed college as a valuable period of exploration. They were anxious to get their degree and get on with the tasks at hand. They believed in themselves and in the myriad of opportunities awaiting their presence. A college degree was the calling card that would allow them onto the playing field, facilitating their rise to dominance and comfort.

Busters, pessimistic about the coming years and with no real sense of direction or enthusiasm for their adult years, have no sense of urgency about completing their education and moving on. Many Busters hope that by relaxing the pace of their program, and maybe by integrating some real-world, non-classroom experiences into their backgrounds, they will be better able to make the crucial decisions about what to be when they grow up.

More Education, Less Smarts

At the same time that young Americans are more likely to earn a college degree, studies also show that they are emerging with fewer tangible skills and less knowledge than in years past. A significant share of the blame is often laid at the feet of the public schools, which appear to be less proficient at educating the new generation.

It would be unfair, of course, to lay the full blame for this poor preparation solely at the feet of the public schools. The other sources of young people's education have also suffered setbacks. For instance, families appear to be providing less educational support than in the past. Churches reach comparatively few young people these days with their message of hope and morality. The input that seems to have an increasing influence—the visual media, television and movies—has provided little in the way of positive values and traditional educational assistance.

Regardless of the reasons, though, the facts are undeniable: our young adults may have invested the required amounts of time, but they graduate from high school with poor study and reasoning skills, tenuous work habits, few non-materialistic goals for the future, and limited factual knowledge.

Educators have subjected students in a variety of countries to similar tests in the areas of math and science. The results consistently show American students lagging in these comparisons, and losing ground over time. The most recent of these comparisons involves the Busters—a generation well-heeled but poorly tutored.

Table 7.2

Proportion of Correct Answers to the Literacy Test Regarding History

topical area of testing	% correct
identification of maps and geography	71%
knowledge of important historical figures	62
knowledge about the Constitution	54
events from World War II through the present	54
dates of key historical events	51
facts related to demographics and migration	51
events of the Reconstruction through World War I era	50
pre-Colonial history	49

Source: What Do Our 17-Year-Olds Know?, Diane Ravitch and Chester Finn, Jr., Perennial Library, New York, 1988, pages 85-120.

Recent studies also show that the crisis is not limited to the areas of math and science. Our young people fare no better when it comes to knowing key facts about history and literature. One of the most reliable and insightful tools in this regard was the national test of eleventh graders conducted by the Foundations for Literacy campaign. In this massive, well-developed study of 7,812 high school students in the areas of history and literature, the results showed that only 54% of the students' replies to multiple-choice questions about history were correctly answered; and just 52% of the questions pertaining to literature were correctly answered. No matter what scale you utilize, these are failing marks.

Table 7.3

Proportion of Correct Answers to the Literacy Test Regarding Literature

topical area of testing	% correct
Shakespeare	68%
literature of the Bible	67
identifying passages and quotations	60
classical mythology and literature	56
historical documents and non-fiction	55
poetry and poets	49
short stories	46
novels and novelists	45
plays and playwrights	44

Source: What Do Our 17-Year-Olds Know?, Diane Ravitch and Chester Finn, Jr., Perennial Library, New York, 1988, pages 85-120.

Having Their Cake

Perhaps the Busters are not energized by the educational process, and look upon their classroom experiences as a necessary means to an end. You can bet that most Busters have a more refined sense of what they want out of a career than what they hope to achieve by attending college.

Busters are in no danger of becoming a welfare class. Currently, among Busters 18 or older, 83% of the males hold a job and 69% of the women do so as well. As America labors through the transition from a manufacturing to a service-based economy, Busters recognize that they are likely to be in demand, for simple demographic reasons if nothing else.

The expectations in some ways mirror the energy fueling the aggressiveness of the Boomers. Nationwide studies among graduating college students conducted by the University of Michigan indicate that Busters are increasingly interested in obtaining jobs that offer a good chance for advancement and promotion, a chance to earn lofty salaries, a chance to get involved in the decision-making apparatus of the organization, and a chance to reflect high status or prestige. They are less likely than previous graduates to exhibit an interest in making a lasting contribution to society through their work.

> **"...the difference between Boomers and Busters may be summed up in this statement: Boomers live to work, while Busters work to live."**

But the difference between Boomers and Busters may be summed up in this statement: Boomers live to work, while Busters work to live. The critical distinction is that Boomers, to an even greater extent than their parents, derive their self-image and self-worth from what they accomplish on the job. They view excellence in work as their ticket to all-out pursuit of leisure as a means of regeneration. The typical Boomer would rather chase the dream of corporate ascension than reallocate resources to achieve balance in life.

Busters gain their stability and energy from non-occupational pursuits. Leisure, flexibility, independence and recreation are of the utmost importance to them. Having watched the burnout pace and vacuous values of the Boomers run that generation ragged for the better part of the last two decades, the Busters have concluded that there must be more to life than a 14-hour-a-day grind. Accordingly, they have rejected the Boomers' model for life: hot pursuit of career dreams, workaholism, title-envy, corporate politicking, and relational and family sacrifices made in return for occupational gain.

Typically, Busters blend their views on an inclusive lifestyle with the realization that they are a necessary, if not exactly treasured, commodity in the labor force. Consequently, they expect the benefits of an executive position without having to pay the dues that precede the reception of such a position. Thus, it would not be uncommon to find a Buster who holds an entry-level position expecting to be included in upper-level decision making processes.

Busters will find the corporate world a hostile environment because they reject one of the most pervasive tenets of corporate America: the chain-of-command authority structure. Busters loathe overt power and authority. Given their views about the value of the world system they will someday inherit, they see organizational hierarchies as insensitive, anachronistic channels of management. They believe that they have useful insights to offer and cannot believe that "working their way up the ladder" will make what they have to offer more valuable.

Busters also thrive in circumstances where a flatter, team-oriented approach exists, enabling every worker to contribute something of unique value to the aggregate process. The team structure allows them to ask their favorite question: "why?" Knowing the rationale behind decisions and feeling as if they have played a role in the development of a plan they will have to implement is one of the best means of persuading and motivating Busters to pour themselves into a project. This is just one example of how Busters prefer to be in a relaxed environment, instead of the button-up, starched-shirt atmosphere that has excited many Builders and Boomers.

Employers who have not comprehended the Buster view of authority frequently become frustrated or even enraged by the behavior and performance of these young employees. Managers who come from the Boomer generation, in particular, are baffled by Busters. Boomers have always assumed that the way they operate is the only feasible way to do it, and therefore assume that other people behave in similar and predictable ways. When Boomers conflict with corporate authority figures, their usual strategy is to argue the merits of their position in the hope of convincing the powers-that-be of their correctness. (Note, of course, that this differs dramatically from the compliant employee mold of the Builders, who "worked through channels" to foster change.)

Busters play the game entirely differently. Lacking a sense of commitment to job, to company, and even to their fellow workers, they simply ignore authority. They do not debate the issue; they quietly pursue their own strategies in their own timing, seemingly oblivious to the environment and demands around them. This approach is based on their determination to engage only in those efforts which hold high promise of resulting in sufficient personal benefit to justify the effort.

> **"Their skills are limited. Attitudinally, they are hard to comprehend. They are often seen as flakes and ingrates. They are difficult to manage because they operate with a different set of core values and perspectives."**

Builders and Boomers view this approach to occupational growth as suicidal. But they generally misinterpret the strategy as one based on ignorance. It is not. The situation is like the difference between Apple and IBM computers: they run on different operating systems. To make either one function effectively, the person in control must master the operational assumptions on which the system (i.e. generation) is based.

Realize that Busters are a new breed of employee:

➤ they hold a different view of their potential—less optimistic about future outcomes and opportunities;

➤ Busters have lesser financial and familial pressures because they graduate from college owing less, they are more likely to live at home during their first years in the work place, and they are less likely to be married before they reach their mid-twenties;

➤ and they have a different emotional bond to job and employer—that is, minimal loyalty, with an easy acceptance of high job turnover and transience.

One recent study suggested that Busters have no corporate umbilical cord: they are expected to change careers (not just employers, mind you, but career paths) up to six times during their working years.

Not Much of a Deal

Employers may view the hiring of Busters as an unattractive deal. Their commitments are short-term. Their skills are limited. Attitudinally, they are hard to comprehend. They are often seen as flakes and ingrates. They are difficult to manage because they operate with a different set of core values and perspectives.

Major corporations have realized that to reach their goals, they must hire and rely upon Busters. It is a marriage of necessity rather than desirability. But in coping with this reality, they have discovered some ways of optimizing the situation.

McDonald's, for instance, is the nation's largest employer of Busters. They have incorporated a system whereby they train all employees in a series of common skills that can be used at all levels of the company's endeavors. Their focus is upon process rather than information. That is, they teach people how to think rather than what to think.

Chrysler is pursuing a similar end. This year the company will spend over $130 million educating its employees. More than 10% of that budget will be allocated to providing their workers with basic literacy skills. Much of the remainder will address procedures and systematic thinking.

At the same time, many of the large and profitable companies in America are re-examining their management and leadership processes. Some of this has been in response to the challenges brought on by the Buster generation. Corporate hierarchies are transitioning from the traditional vertical hierarchy to a more horizontal, team-driven style. In many instances, it is not only the Busters that thrive in such an environment, but older employees as well.

BEHIND *The Facade*

Sherri Winston ◆ Age: 19

She attends a state university now, having transferred in upon completing a two-year course of study at her local community college. Sherri is not sure what she wants to be when she grows up. Well, she'll tell you what she wants to be, but the chances are good that the choice will change within the next month or so.

"When I went to college, at first I thought I would get prepped for law school. But I took a few low-level law classes—you know, environmental law, business law, family and the law—and just didn't like it. I couldn't see myself buried in books for the rest of my life arguing about history and people's past problems."

She has been through a series of changes in her major course of study. After law it was business, then sociology, then psychology, then communications. Currently she is exploring journalism.

"I like knowing what's going on in the world and expressing my opinions about it. Working in the electronic media would be exciting."

She, like most of her fellow students, feels as if additional education is not an option.

"You can't get anywhere without some college training. You look at the stats and it seems that even a B.A. isn't enough anymore. But the thought

of spending even more time in the classroom..." Her voice trails off as she deals with the mental anguish of such a thought.

Sherri believes that her parents did little to prepare her for life after high school.

"Mom and Dad both worked full-time. The kids were kind of a night time chore they were obligated to deal with. They never gave me a solid direction to consider. It was always, 'go where your heart is, Sherri. You'll never be happy unless you follow your heart.' I'm like, 'What? What does that mean?'

That's why college has been so difficult for me. I feel like I'm a stranger in a foreign land, trying to cope with choices but lacking the perspective I need to make sense of it all. I just don't know what it's supposed to be like."

> ## "I couldn't see myself buried in books for the rest of my life arguing about history and people's past problems."

Examining her curriculum is a fascinating trip through the maze of her emotions at a given point in her short college career. She has hopscotched through several majors and a bunch of the required core courses—and has studiously avoided courses in which she has no interest, such as the physical sciences, foreign languages, and mathematics.

What will probably happen after graduating?

"Oh, I'm sure I'll have several major career shifts before I retire. I'm not really set on any career, and I'd probably get bored with one career after a few years anyway. It's important to me that I enjoy what I'm doing and get a sense of significance out of my work. Money is important, but it's not all there is to a job. Maybe I'll change my mind on that, but for now, I want a job that allows me to ask questions and get real answers."

EIGHT

People in Perspective

IF NOTHING ELSE ABOUT THE BUSTERS APPEALS TO YOU, PERHAPS you can appreciate one major departure of theirs from the dominant Boomer mentality: people matter.

One of the most striking elements in the world view of Boomers has been their unspoken perception of other people as a means to an end. As one advertising executive described the Boomers, "they are the first generation to care more about the products they buy than about the people who manufactured those products."

Busters, in comparison to the preceding generation, are more emotionally sensitive and more relational in character. They are more interested in developing and nurturing long-lasting, symbiotic relationships. Although interpersonal relationships are not the driving force in their lives, Busters do demonstrate a greater willingness to sacrifice some of their time and energy to initiate and nurture meaningful friendships.

The impetus behind this may have to do with their own poverty of emotional connections as they were raised. Busters tended to be raised in a more isolated environment due to divorce, household transience, their own diminished communication skills, and the dissolution of neighborhoods. As they matured, they tended to place greater emphasis upon enjoying and mastering technology than upon the pursuit of human interaction, a behavior affirmed by their parents' desire to see results rather than relationships as the product of their days' efforts.

Today, though, Busters see friends and family as two of the more important aspects of their lives. When they reflect on their sources of emotional support and encouragement, about two out of three Busters claim that they often receive such help from personal friends (67%) and from family members (62%). All other sources of support pale in comparison.

The Role of Friendships

If you were to chart how Busters use their time, you'd discover that they spend the largest proportions of their waking hours on employment, eating meals, and watching television. Apart from these endeavors, their most prolific investment of time is in friendships. It appears that Busters allocate an average of about one hour a day to maintaining their relationships with non-family individuals. This may not sound like much, but it is a significant rise from the amount of time the typical Boomer set aside for similar activities when they were at the same stage in the life cycle.

Busters are picky about whom they invite into their lives. In general, their friends are a select group of individuals, hand-picked for the common interests they share and the comfortable conversation and activity that unfolds. Notice that while Busters spend comparatively more time with friends, their choice of friends (and, to some extent, their involvement with those friends) is based upon what they expect will be a fair exchange.

Random or chance encounters with other adults have little opportunity to dent the Busters' daily agenda. For instance, neighbors get little attention—an average of less than five minutes per week. People encountered at a church or religious center frequented by Busters also get minimal amounts of the Busters' time: less than 10 minutes per week. Interaction with co-workers consumes roughly an hour per work day. The rest of the relational time is devoted to family and personal friends of their choosing.

Table 8.1
Sources of Help and Encouragement

source of encouragement	how often each provided such support			
	often	sometimes	not too often	never
personal friends	67%	23%	5%	2%
immediate family	62	22	8	5
the Bible	22	26	19	31
books, other than Bible	18	19	23	38
minister or priest	15	20	20	43
boss or employer	15	15	21	46
tapes by leaders	5	17	12	64
a professional counselor	2	13	16	66

Source: Barna Research Group, Ltd.

The most satisfying relationships of all tend to come from family. One-quarter of the Busters claim their most fulfilling relationship is with their spouse (23%); one out of eight cites his or her relationship with their children (13%); an equivalent proportion mention other relatives (12%); and 5% cite both their spouse and children as their choice. Overall, then, more than half (53%) list family members as their closest confidantes. In comparison, 42% of the Busters mention personal friends as their most satisfying relationships.

The power of friendships among Busters should not be underestimated. When they engage in their favorite leisure activity, the majority of these young adults (53%) do so along with their friends. Smaller percentages of Busters describe their favorite leisure pursuit as one which involves their family (39%) or which they do solo (29%).

Where do Busters make the contacts that eventually become lasting friends? The most common places are work (cited by

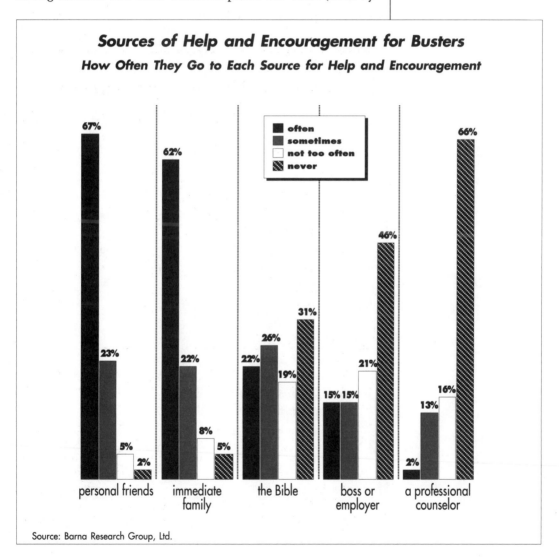

Sources of Help and Encouragement for Busters

How Often They Go to Each Source for Help and Encouragement

Legend:
- often
- sometimes
- not too often
- never

personal friends: 67%, 23%, 5%, 2%
immediate family: 62%, 22%, 8%, 5%
the Bible: 22%, 26%, 19%, 31%
boss or employer: 15%, 15%, 21%, 46%
a professional counselor: 2%, 13%, 16%, 66%

Source: Barna Research Group, Ltd.

42%) and school (38%). Busters are much less likely than other adults to view church as a source of friendships (29% do so) and much more likely to perceive social and fitness clubs as a major source. Reflecting one of the cultural phenomena that emerged during their time, Busters, alone, described shopping malls as another high-profile source of friendships.

Nearly half of the generation wishes they had more close friends. It's not that it seems difficult to actually make deep, lasting relationships. They view the process of connecting and maintaining the connection as quite feasible. The difficulty seems to be how to handle time and circumstances. With the crush of opportunities and obligations cascading upon them, Busters struggle to balance the myriad of competing time demands.

Table 8.2
How Busters Feel about Friendships

statement about friendships	agree	disagree
• it's easy for you to make deep, lasting friendships	69%	30%
• you wish you had more close friends	44	55
• if a person does not have friends, it's their own fault	41	58
• you don't personally know anyone who is truly lonely	29	70
• it's nearly impossible to have long-lasting friendships these days	28	72
• in times of trouble, you do not have anyone you can turn to for real comfort or support	9	90

Source: Barna Research Group, Ltd.

Although nine out of ten Busters say they have one or more people they can turn to for help or comfort in times of trouble, most of them admit to knowing people who are truly lonely. And they are reluctant to hold those individuals responsible for their loneliness; six out of ten Busters concur that it is probably not that person's own fault that they are lonely.

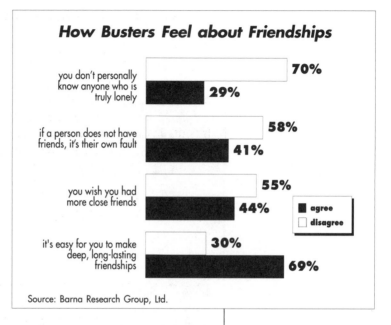

How Busters Feel about Friendships

you don't personally know anyone who is truly lonely — 70% / 29%

if a person does not have friends, it's their own fault — 58% / 41%

you wish you had more close friends — 55% / 44%

■ agree
□ disagree

it's easy for you to make deep, long-lasting friendships — 30% / 69%

Source: Barna Research Group, Ltd.

The challenge for Busters is to make time work in their favor in the initiation and nurturing of true friendships. Toward that end, many of the Busters have attempted to substitute "quality time" for the amount of time they might ideally like to spend in pursuit of special friendships. However, until they sort out the relational pressures, nine out of ten Busters are relying upon the quality time concept as a means of justifying their limited involvement in certain relationships.

What Is a Family?

When you begin to understand how Busters define "family," you start to comprehend why family systems in America are changing so dramatically. In fact, the distinction between friends and family gets blurred pretty quickly.

Most Busters believe that "family" refers to any of several different types or forms of relationships. For instance, about one out of every four Busters describes family in each of the following ways:

- people with whom you have close relationships
  or deep personal/emotional bonds 28%
- those individuals with whom you have a mutual
  personal commitment or love relationship 25
- your good friends, those with whom you are
  compatible, those with whom there is
  mutual caring 24
- the people who are there for you to provide help
  or emotional support, as needed 23
- people who are related by marriage 21
- individuals to whom you are closely related,
  by marriage or blood lines 19

An additional 11% say that people who live together, regardless of their legal status, form a family unit. Nine percent have a relatively encompassing definition, stating that all people with whom you have significant interaction can be deemed family.

Busters, then, are less interested in traditional perspectives, legal definitions, and religious assumptions regarding family. Their dominant criterion for determining family membership has to do with depth of bonding or personal commitment. While our research did not explore this possibility, it seems reasonable to expect that some Busters would go so far as to say that people who are legally bound in matrimony but do not like each other or share meaningful experiences together are not a family—regardless of what the wedding certificate or Census Bureau may claim.

This Nineties view on family fits well with the Buster view of the world. Old values and definitions did not work. Rigid classification schemes offer little value. Perceptual homogeneity suffocates people's hopes and dreams and is not a priority. To Busters, family is a viable concept only if defined in broad terms. This is partly due to their experience, partly related to their goals and expectations for the future, and partly reflective of their emerging vision of a new social order which they will help create.

When Busters are pushed to refine their perceptions of where "family" stops and "friendships" set in, the line is drawn pretty far from where it might have been drawn just thirty years ago. For example, Builders viewed co-habiting hetero-sexuals as "people living in sin." A large proportion (42%) of Busters (for whom the concept of sin is, at best, fuzzy), would describe an unmarried couple living together, without children, as a family. Add children to the same situation and the proportion doubles: 82% consider this household a family. In the same manner, nine out of ten adults (89%) view a single parent and his or her child as a family. Marriage, obviously, is not the determinant of family in the Buster mindset.

Perhaps most astonishing is the widespread acceptance among Busters of gay households. Two people of the same gender living in the same home and having a sexual relationship with each other are construed as a family by one-fourth of the Busters (26%). While only one-tenth as many Busters claim they have actually engaged in homosexual sexual activity, the openness to such lifestyles as legitimate family units is significantly greater than among the Builders (20%) and Seniors (13%).

While these views about family represent a dramatic shift from what was believed a few decades ago, it is useful to know that Busters are not alone in their strikingly different views about family. While they are somewhat more likely to define families in novel ways, they are not too different from Boomers, are noticeably but not radically different from Builders, and bear the least resemblance to Seniors. Even many Seniors, however, seem to have caught the new vision for family systems and have taken to accepting the majority view as their own.

The Path to a Pluralist Perception

How did the views of Busters become so open to various family forms? Some clues can be found by studying those entities which the Busters themselves point to as shaping influences.

A survey conducted in the summer of 1992 indicated that of seven potential influences on people's thinking and actions related to family, Busters felt the most impactive factors were the views transmitted by the mass media and the increase in the number of working women. Fewer Busters identified the other five factors as exerting a lot of influence: the lifestyles of entertainers, government policies, school policies and teaching, and the declining levels of public involvement in Christianity.

A separate study conducted during the spring of the same year discovered that other comparatively influential elements were one's personal family experiences (e.g. marriage, raising children) and personal religious beliefs and experiences.

Table 8.3

Factors That Have Had "a Lot" of Influence on People's Thinking and Behavior Related to Family

source of influence	Busters	others
• the mass media	26%	31%
• increased number of working women	26	30
• the lifestyles of entertainers	12	22
• government policies and laws	12	14
• the teaching and beliefs of churches and religious leaders	12	13
• policies and teaching about family in the public schools	11	14
• changes in people's levels of involvement in Christianity	9	16

Source: Barna Research Group, Ltd.

Busters readily admit that they are often perplexed by the decisions they must make regarding family. There are a number of different sources of insight to which they might turn for assistance. Importantly, none of those sources is recognized by the entire generation as being authoritative, nor is there any single source which Busters would consistently view as having all the wisdom they need in any given situation.

The sources of value listed by the largest number of Busters were their personal religious beliefs (mentioned as being very helpful on family decisions by 26%), the Bible (28%), and their relatives (24%). The statistics related to religious beliefs and the Bible are unexpectedly high, given the restrained religious involvement and fervor of this generation. What makes them even more astounding is that Busters were higher than the Boomers and equivalent to Builders and Seniors regarding their likelihood of turning to the Bible for family advice.

In context, these percentages show that only a small segment of the Busters view religious sources as being truly helpful in family matters. However, in relation to the other sources of advice and assistance available, religious guides emerged as remarkably reliable and helpful sources in the eyes of the broadest coalition of young adults.

As for the high rating ascribed to relatives, Busters were over 50% more likely to cite relatives as a very helpful resource on such matters than were people from any of the other generations interviewed.

The next echelon of trusted sources of help included books (18%), friends (17%), psycholo-

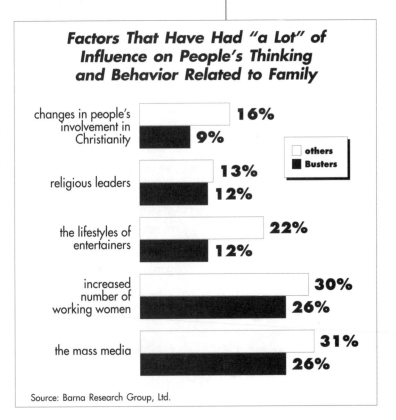

Factors That Have Had "a Lot" of Influence on People's Thinking and Behavior Related to Family

changes in people's involvement in Christianity — others **16%** / Busters **9%**

religious leaders — others **13%** / Busters **12%**

the lifestyles of entertainers — others **22%** / Busters **12%**

increased number of working women — others **30%** / Busters **26%**

the mass media — others **31%** / Busters **26%**

Source: Barna Research Group, Ltd.

gists and counselors (15%), and local religious leaders (13%). Lowest on the list of trusted advisers in family matters were television programs (9%) and government policies or resources (3%).

Busters are, indeed, the television generation. Although a comparatively small percentage of young adults cited television as a viable resource in family decision-making, they were three times more likely than Seniors to mention television as potentially a very helpful source, and nine times more likely than either Boomers or Builders. Stated differently, of all of the adults who deem television to be a very helpful resource in family matters, 50% of them are Busters—even though Busters represent only 15% of the adult population.

Table 8.4
Sources of Help in Making Decisions about Family Matters

source of help	Busters	Boomers	Builders	Seniors
the Bible	28%	22%	30%	29%
your religious beliefs	26	22	33	31
relatives	24	15	16	17
books, other than the Bible	18	13	15	13
friends	17	13	16	18
psychologists or counselors	15	9	10	12
local religious leaders	13	10	14	13
television programs	9	1	1	3
government policies or laws	3	2	2	4

Source: Barna Research Group, Ltd.

Will Marriage Survive?

The trend regarding the diminished importance of marriage is undeniable. Over the last two decades, fewer adults have chosen to become or remain married. Whereas nearly eight out of ten adults over age 25 were married in previous decades, that figure has dropped to just six out of ten adults these days.

Busters, though, believe that marriage is a good thing. Most Busters either are married now (30%), definitely want to be (30%), or would like to be if the right person came along (29%). Very few Busters believe that marriage is an outdated social institution (11%). And just two out of ten Busters say it is better to remain single than to get married.

Why would Busters want to be married if they have seen so many broken marriages and broken hearts resulting from bad marriages? The desire for lasting companionship tops the list of compelling reasons. Nearly six out of ten single Busters say their primary desire for marrying would be to gain the companionship of the other person. Other powerful reasons for talking a walk down the aisle are to have children (listed by 27%), to share their love with another person (26%), to gain a greater measure of stability or security in life (20%), and to be part of a family (10%).

In the back of many Busters' minds, though, lurks the specter of potential divorce. As the generation that has been most widely victimized by the difficulties of divorce, Busters perceive divorce as an ugly but inescapable reality for many marriages. Although no Buster has reached the age of 30 yet, and not even one-third of them have been married, 6% of the 18- to 26-year-olds have already been through a divorce. Many more will follow suit.

> **"Yet, regardless of what God intended, many Busters (27%) assert that these days one ought not to think of marriage as a permanent arrangement between individuals."**

One-quarter of all Busters (24%) believe that anyone getting married these days should expect to get divorced. More than one out of three say it is nearly impossible to have a successful marriage anymore (35%). And most striking of all is the reality that six out of every ten Busters (61%) believe that in the future, most adults will wind up divorced within their first five years of marriage. In response to the increasing probability that they and their friends will experience a shattered marriage, nearly half of all Busters (43%) would like to see conditions changed to make it more difficult to get a divorce.

The Busters' attitudes toward marriage, in general, reflect a blend of traditional and contemporary perspectives. Most Busters believe that God intended marriages to last for a lifetime (85%). And while we cannot say that most Busters are necessarily romantics, the data clearly indicate that they view love as the proper force behind a marriage; only 7% said it is okay to marry someone for money or something other than love.

Yet, regardless of what God intended, many Busters (27%) assert that these days one ought not to think of marriage as a permanent arrangement between individuals. Most of them would contend that marriage does increase family stability (59%), but that you are setting yourself at risk by building your life around the marriage. Consequently, the utilitarian view emerges: three out of every four Busters say that one should not let a marriage limit their opportunities and activities in life (74%). Rather, marriage is a social crutch that facilitates a more successful romp through the dangers and potentials of a competitive, complicated world.

Yet another *nouveau* idea is the belief that gay marriages are acceptable unions. Among Busters, one-quarter (25%) said that there is nothing wrong with allowing two people of the same gender to marry each other.

Many Busters also accept the practice of co-habitation as either a substitute for, or precursor to, marriage. Although government statistics have shown that people who co-habit prior to getting married actually have about an 80% higher chance of getting divorced than do those individuals who never live together before exchanging vows, six out of ten Busters (60%) believe it is best to co-habit before marriage. Half of the Busters (50%) go so far as to state that they expect co-habitation to replace marriage. This makes sense in light of the 70% of all Busters who say that fewer people will be getting married by the year 2000.

Busters as Parents

George Gerbner, the communications researcher at the University of Pennsylvania who has spent the last two decades studying the effects of television on America, has some unkind words for today's parents, many of whom are Busters.

"Three out of four American kids grow up today in a home without a full-time parent, but with a television set that is on an average of seven hours a day. Most stories about life and values are not told by parents, grandparents, teachers, clergy or others with their own stories to tell, but by a handful of distant conglomerates with something to sell. The average ten-year-old can name more brands of beer than Presidents." (1)

Will Busters follow the footsteps of the Boomers in their parenting behavior? Boomers were the first generation not to promise their children that they would pass their wealth on upon their death. Busters harbor substantial resentment toward their parents because they feel their elders did not teach them how to learn, or how to cope with failure, or how to be responsible citizens.

Busters possess what appears to be a realistic view of the joys and frustrations of parenting these days. A healthy proportion (30%) claim that raising children is not as much fun these days as it was in the past. They acknowledge that kids are influenced by schools, government, the media and other sources more than by parents (77% say this is true).

What we may well witness in the next 15 years is a partial restoration of traditional household configurations, as the Busters react to the hurts and sorrows they suffered as the children of divorce, workaholics, and impersonal parents. The attitudes of Busters about parenting point toward a preference for less risky, experimental and selfish parenting behaviors.

Two-thirds of the Busters (65%) say that a home in which the dad works full-time and the mother is a homemaker is more likely to be a happy family than if both parents work. Realize, of course, that most of the Busters answering these questions were raised in homes in which both parents worked or in homes with a single parent.

The Mr. Mom concept has not captured the imagination of the generation. Seven out of ten Busters (71%) believe that a family would be happier if the mother, rather than the father, stays home with the children while the other spouse earns the income.

As for the care of the children, Busters do not have a sanguine view of day care arrangements. Six out of ten Busters (57%) say a family would be happier if one parent stays home full-time and the family has to sacrifice its standard of living than for both parents to work and place the children in a good day care center. Busters would prefer leaving their children with relatives to enrolling them in day care (71%), but neither is as desirable as one of the adults being a full-time parent.

> **"Seven out of ten Busters (71%) believe that a family would be happier if the mother, rather than the father, stays home with the children while the other spouse earns the income."**

In practical terms, this may not be easy to pull off. Attitudes aside, there has been a whopping increase in the number of births to unwed mothers in the 15- to 24-year-old age bracket. Since 1970, in fact, the number of such births each year has more than doubled—even though there are fewer women in that age cohort today. Each year we have well over 600,000 new births to unmarried females who are in the Baby Bust segment. (This does not include the 500,000-plus legal abortions performed on Buster women each year.)

Young adults also understand the persuasion game. Ask them who should have "a lot" of responsibility for teaching values to children, and you hear the expected replies. Ninety eight percent list parents; 56% say the schools; 51% mention churches; 28% say the friends or peers of their children; 12% point to government policies and regulations for such help; just 9% identify the media as desirable perpetrators of values. In fact, 95% say that the single entity which should have the greatest degree of influence should be parents.

But ask them who does have the most influence on kids values these days and the nod goes to friends and peers (mentioned by 39%) and the media (24%). Only 21% proclaim that parents do, in reality, have the most significant influence on today's youngsters.

Most Busters do admit that if you want to be a good parent, you must spend a lot of time with your children each day (79%). The question is: will they?

Sex Is Hot

Table 8.5
Should Schools Teach Abstinence or 'Safe Sex'?

preferred school position	Busters	Boomers	Builders	Seniors
• encourage no sex until married	19%	39%	52%	58%
• encourage using a condom	69	51	32	30
• teach both responses	5	6	9	6
• use other, better solutions	7	3	4	5
• don't know what to do	*	2	3	1

* indicates less than one-half of 1%

Source: Barna Research Group, Ltd.

The sexual desires and activity of Busters do not seem much different from that of their predecessors. Perhaps this is due to the training and example they received from their parents. Several years ago, Peter Hart conducted a study for *Rolling Stone* magazine among Boomers. He learned that most of them had engaged in sexual intercourse before marriage, but only 8% of them said they regretted having done so. It seems feasible to expect that the Boomers, then, would pass on a less conservative or less traditional sexual value system to their children.

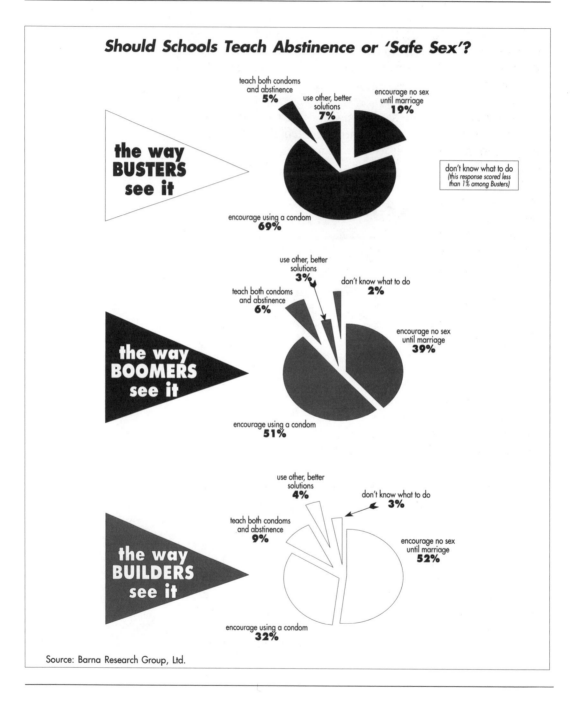

Should Schools Teach Abstinence or 'Safe Sex'?

the way BUSTERS see it

teach both condoms and abstinence
5%

use other, better solutions
7%

encourage no sex until marriage
19%

don't know what to do
(this response scored less than 1% among Busters)

encourage using a condom
69%

the way BOOMERS see it

use other, better solutions
3%

don't know what to do
2%

teach both condoms and abstinence
6%

encourage no sex until marriage
39%

encourage using a condom
51%

the way BUILDERS see it

use other, better solutions
4%

don't know what to do
3%

teach both condoms and abstinence
9%

encourage no sex until marriage
52%

encourage using a condom
32%

Source: Barna Research Group, Ltd.

Television and movies have also transmitted a new world view of sexual activity. Recent studies have shown that most of the instances of implied sexual intercourse on television occur between unmarried adults. Movies reflect the same behavior, perhaps in a more vivid fashion.

Almost half of all live births to Baby Buster females last year (47%) were to those who were unmarried. This is the highest proportion ever recorded for women in the 15- to 24-year age category. The trend line shows a strong upward movement.

One-third of the Busters (31%) assert that "it is very unlikely for a male and female to have a lasting friendship without it becoming a sexual relationship." Indeed, the experience of Busters to date proves the point. Two out of ten Busters who are currently single have had intercourse with a married person; one out of every fourteen married Busters has done the same. And among single Busters, more than three-quarters claim that they have engaged in sexual intercourse with other single adults. Today, only 23% of the single Busters profess to being virgins.

Not even the AIDS scare has altered their feelings about sex. When asked what the most reasonable course of action for the public schools would be—to encourage teenagers not to have sex (i.e. abstinence) or to encourage them to use condoms (i.e. "safe sex")—Busters advocate encouraging condom use by a four to one margin. Among older adults, the preference is different: 47% said the schools should preach abstinence, 40% suggested encouraging condom use. Boomers, by the way, while not as supportive of condom use instead of abstinence, were the only generation to share the Busters' preference.

Gay Rights

Busters also possess a more "liberal" view of gay rights. Relatively few Busters admit to having participated in gay sex: 3%, mostly comprised of women. However, the Busters' prevailing views on homosexuality reflect the changing national acceptance of gay lifestyles and practices.

Only one-third of the Busters (32%) buy the recent research suggesting that people are born homosexual. A slight majority (55%) believe that gay sex is immoral. Half say that opposition to gay rights and lifestyles is evidence of being "closed-minded" and half say that such opposition is not being closed-minded.

But the prevailing Buster view of the world—that there is no absolute truth, so people should be allowed to do whatever they want as long as it does not harm others—emerges on gay rights and lifestyles issues. More than four out of every ten Busters (44%) said that gay couples should be allowed to get married. Nearly as many (38%) felt that they should also be allowed to adopt and raise children.

In the days ahead, most Busters (71%) foresee expanded rights for gay adults. The growing support of gay rights among Busters, though, is more likely a philosophical decision than a matter of going with the societal flow.

What's Coming for the Family?

If Busters are right, we ought not to expect a return to the traditional family values of the Fifties. Less than one out of every six Busters predicts such a shift in values.

What, then, will we witness? If Busters have their way—and, as the emerging generation of parents, chances are better-than-even that what they expect is what will transpire—you might anticipate a uniquely Buster family philosophy to take root in America. Only 15% say they are betting on a return to traditional values. Even fewer (10%) expect the family values currently in place to prevail over the next two decades. The vast majority of young adults are looking forward to a new combination of traditional and contemporary values that has not yet been defined.

This view speaks to the deep-seated dismay Busters harbor regarding both their own upbringing and the family models displayed for them by their immediate predecessors. Busters will again demonstrate their innovative skills by creating a new core of family values developed on-the-job. New models will be born, bearing limited resemblance to those attempted by the Boomers. The one soothing thought resting in the back of the Busters' minds is that no matter what new systems and models they generate, they feel they cannot do any worse than the Boomers did.

BEHIND
The Facade

Kevin Larkin ◆ Age: 24

Kevin Larkin and his female friend, Kristina Shales, have been living together for seven months now. It is not an arrangement that has pleased either of their parents.

> *"My mom freaked out when I broke the news to her. But she'll get over it. This is the Nineties. You're out of line if you don't live together first."*

They say they expect to get married some day, but that there is no hurry. They allow that they may even have a child together before they exchange vows.

> *"It's a very serious decision, having kids. Much more serious than getting married. But it's also a decision that will help us determine if marriage is the thing for us."*

When the issue of sexual purity is raised, they both chuckle politely.

> *"I lost my virginity when I was 14,"* Kristina proclaims without a hint of either sorrow or boasting. *"It didn't make me a whore, or immoral. It made me one of the girls. Geez, I wasn't even one of the first."*

And there have been many partners along the way since then.

> **"...I'm sure I'll be married someday. But it's more of a nuisance, an old people's thing."**

"Yeah, I've been real lucky not to have contracted anything. That's one of the great things about living with Kevin. We have agreed not to sleep with other people. I feel safe with him, in many ways."

Safe enough to get married?

"What's the rush? We've made our commitment to each other for the time being. Running down the aisle won't improve our relationship."

Kevin somehow feels uncomfortable with marriage.

"I believe in it and I'm sure I'll be married someday. But it's more of a nuisance, an old people's thing, than something that will really upgrade my life. When it's time to get married, I'm sure I'll know. For now, life is good. Our relationship is cool and I'm in no hurry to ruin a good thing."

Tales of Sin, Salvation & Self

IT IS NOT UNUSUAL FOR YOUNG ADULTS TO DEMONSTRATE a studied indifference to organized religion. For many decades, sociologists and religious leaders have pondered the significance of the move away from religious study and practice among our young adults. The general conclusion is that "this, too, shall pass"; as young adults mature, they, like their parents and grandparents before them, will return to religion for the virtues and solace it offers. The determined avoidance of organized religion during the late teens and early twenties is not so much a reasoned and impassioned resistance to God or other spiritual realities as a flexing of their independence from the older generations and their prevailing models of structure, authority and order.

Will the Baby Busters follow the same pattern, ignoring or dismissing organized religion in the Nineties, only to begin the pilgrimage back in the early part of the next century? Based on their underlying attitudes and values, it is reasonable to assume that Busters will return to organized religion. But it also seems likely that when they return, they will come back to different faiths than their parents associated with, and that they will assert their uniqueness by participating in a significant restructuring of the forms and formats of organized religion in the opening years of the next century.

The journey, though, will probably be unique and unpredictable in its nuances as is so much of the Buster experience and lifestyle.

Exposing Themselves to God

Busters may be less involved in organized religion than are their elders, but they do not shun religion. In fact, a majority of Busters are currently active in some type of church or religious group.

Table 9.1
The Religious Activities of Busters in Comparison to Older Adults

religious activity	—in last 7 days—	
	Busters	others
• attended religious worship services	34%	49%
• attended religious instruction	10	24
• read part of the Bible	31	51
• told people with different beliefs about your religious beliefs	36	30

Source: Barna Research Group, Ltd.

One common measure of religious involvement is church attendance. Our studies show that while Busters are less likely to attend church services than are older adults, one-third of them attend during any given week (34%) and half of them attend during the course of a typical month (51%). Busters possess an interest in religion because, in their transaction-driven way of thinking, they see faith systems as potentially providing them with new insights or useful perspectives which would help them cope with life more effectively. But regular church attendance does not fit their present lifestyle or correspond with the magnitude of the spiritual void they feel. As an occasional activity, most Busters perceive churches as offering value.

Consider the frequency with which Busters engage in a variety of religious activities. The statistics suggest that Busters lag their elders in each of the endeavors examined (see Table 9.1)—except discussing what they believe with others. This penchant for mulling over spiritual truths and perceptions is a perfect example of their determination to explore and reconstruct their views on reality, and to try to take others with them in that process.

In a global context, Busters certainly emerge with a different character than they do within a national context. Compared to adults in other nations, especially young adults, this profile rates American Busters as

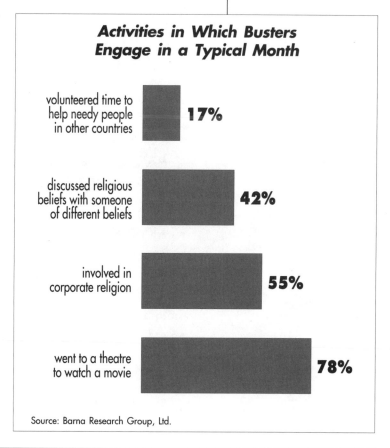

Activities in Which Busters Engage in a Typical Month

volunteered time to help needy people in other countries **17%**

discussed religious beliefs with someone of different beliefs **42%**

involved in corporate religion **55%**

went to a theatre to watch a movie **78%**

Source: Barna Research Group, Ltd.

among the more religious people on the face of the earth today.

In most instances, the gap between the participation levels of the Busters and older adults is very substantial. For instance, when it comes to attending religious services in any given week, Busters are about 30% less likely to do so. They are more than 50% less likely to attend religious instruction classes (e.g. Sunday school). The differential is not as large between Busters and their elders when it comes to monthly religious activity, indicating that the number of times their elders engage in religious efforts is higher.

Our surveys have uncovered a host of other religious activities in which Busters participate, although their involvement levels are (again) below those for older adults in every case. The data, displayed in Table 9.2, show that literally tens of millions of Busters receive monthly exposure to religious teaching and viewpoints (and especially Christian perspectives) through a wide variety of mass media: books, magazines, television, radio, recorded music, audio cassettes and videotapes.

Table 9.2

Religious Activities in Which Busters Engage in a Typical Month

activity	Busters
• watch religious television programs	38%
• listen to radio stations playing Christian music	36
• listen to Christian preaching or teaching on radio	29
• read a Christian book	25
• read a Christian magazine	23
• attend a small group that meets to pray or study the Bible, other than a Sunday school class	14

Source: Barna Research Group, Ltd.

Other measures of religious activity from our surveys posit that about 6% of the Busters are presently involved in teaching a Sunday school class at a church and 7% are involved in the lay leadership of their church.

Notice some of the interesting lifestyle choices and priorities of the Busters. As a population group, they are: more likely to attend movies than religious services; more likely to read books for pleasure than to read the Bible; more likely to enroll in a tuition-based class at an educational institution than to attend free classes at a church; and more likely to participate in a product boycott than to participate in a small group that meets for prayer or Bible study.

> **"By and large Busters describe themselves as Christians and attend either Protestant or Catholic churches."**

Bible reading is an interesting study in itself. The vast majority of Busters (over 80%) own at least one Bible. Considerable proportions of Busters also own Bible reference tools. For instance, 56% said they own a study Bible; 35% claimed to own a Bible dictionary; 28% said they had one or more Bible commentaries; and 9% stated that they own a concordance.

When asking people if they have read the Bible in the past seven days, surveys generally obtain a lower score than when people are asked how many days in a typical week they would read the Bible. In this case, only 23% of the Busters claim they read the Bible in the last seven days (averaged over several surveys during the course of the year); 34% say they have done so in the last 30 days; and 45% say they do so in a typical week.

Among those who read the Bible in a typical week, 18% read from Scripture on one day; 9%, two days; 9%, three to five days; and 5%, six or seven days in a usual week. This reflects less consistency in Bible reading than is true for older adults. And among the Busters who do read the Bible in the course of a week, the cumulative amount of time they devote to that practice is slightly less than one hour.

Busters' responses regarding church attendance patterns parallel those of Bible reading. Thirty-four percent say they have attended a religious service in the last seven days; 51% say they have done so in the last 30 days; and 59% say they usually attend such services at least once a month in a typical month.

Although 41% indicate that they do not attend religious services in a typical month, 15% claim to do so about once a month; 11% do so twice a month; 9% attend three times per month; and 23% attend four or more times per month.

This lukewarm attendance pattern may be partially attributed to the fact that only 19% strongly assert that church attendance is a Biblical mandate. An equal proportion of Busters firmly assert that such attendance is a man-made dictate.

Loyalty to institutions, not one of the attributes for which Busters are well-known, is also absent when it comes to church attendance. Barely half of the young adults (52%) claim that they always attend the same church; one-third (31%) say they usually attend the same church, but sometimes visit others in the area instead; and 10% regularly divide their attendance between two or more churches. The incidence of multiple-church attendance is higher among single Busters than among those who are married.

What types of churches do they attend? By and large, Busters describe themselves as Christians and attend either Protestant or Catholic churches. About three out of ten Busters (29%) go to Catholic churches. About half say they generally attend some type of Protestant church. By the way, 12% say that they have no religious affiliation whatsoever.

The denominational affiliations of Busters show that they are less likely than their parents and grandparents to associate with "mainline Protestant" groups. For instance, only 5% call themselves Methodist; 4% Lutheran; 3% Presbyterian; 2% Church of Christ; and 1% Episcopal. Twenty-one percent described themselves as Baptist. Charismatic denominations such as the Assemblies of God, Foursquare and other Pentecostal churches drew the allegiance of 3%. The largest of the non-Christian religious groups among Busters were the Jewish faith (2% of the Buster segment) and the Mormon church (2%).

About half of the Busters say that religion is very important in their life. This, again, is lower than among older adults

(54%). A similar percentage of Busters (50%) describe themselves as "religious," making this characterization one of the more widely accepted self-descriptions chosen by the Busters.

Religious Beliefs

In general, Busters believe in God: 91% profess to believe in God or a higher power. However, the traditional understanding of God—i.e. one all-powerful God who created the world and rules it today—is believed by less than two-thirds of the Buster generation (64%). Eastern views and "new age" philosophies have shown their greatest in-roads among the Busters. For example, 12% believe that God is the full realization of human potential; 8% claim that God is simply a state of higher consciousness; 4% believe that every human being is his or her own god.

The Buster views of Jesus Christ and their acceptance of evangelical Christian theology is also overtly different from the mainstream perspective. For instance, while more than two-thirds of the pre-Buster population say that they have made "a personal commitment to Jesus Christ that is still important in their life today," this is true among just half of the Baby Busters (54%). And when it comes to beliefs about eternal life, Busters are significantly less likely to believe that they will live eternally because they have "confessed their sins and accepted Jesus Christ as their savior." While this view is ascribed to by about four out of ten pre-Busters, it describes just 29% of the Busters.

Barna Research has used the above definitions of a "born again Christian" for the past decade. Our studies have shown that when the actual term, "born again Christian," is used, it carries so much perceptual and cultural baggage (mostly negative in character) that many individuals who have a vital relationship with Jesus Christ refuse to label themselves as "born again" while many people who don't have a clue about the character, nature or purpose of Christ's life blithely characterize themselves as such. Among the Busters, only one out of every four of the 18- to 26-year-old segment describes themselves as "born again" (25%).

The deeper one digs into the religious beliefs of the Busters, the more apparent it becomes that while millions of Busters attended religious services, classes and events during their formative years, they simply have not embraced much of what they heard, saw, or experienced. Their beliefs represent an astonishing shift from the belief systems of generations preceding them—that is, the very people who conscientiously attempted to pass on the same religious values that the teachers themselves possessed.

Most Busters (though not an overwhelming majority) believe in the Judeo-Christian understanding of a single, omnipotent, holy and eternal God. But there is surprisingly little else that this generation strongly believes from the traditional Christian view.

As seen in Table 9.3 most Busters (62%) strongly believe that God hears people's prayers and has the power to answer them. At the same time, though, one-third of all young adults strongly believe that no matter who people pray to, those prayers are answered by the same god, regardless of the name or identity assigned to that supreme being.

While Christian churches have spent decades teaching and warning people about the evil power and influence of the devil, one-third of the Busters firmly deny the existence of such an evil spirit.

It is a minority of Busters who strongly affirm the inerrancy of the Bible (44%), who strongly feel they have a duty to tell people who believe differently about the content of their own religious beliefs (36%), and who firmly believe that the Christian faith has all the answers to leading a successful life (23%). Although just 9% strongly agree that sin is an outdated concept, less than half (45%) strongly disagree with that notion. Even the venerable Ten Commandments get limited respect from this generation: just 54% strongly disagree that the Law given to Moses is not relevant for people living today. And while many Busters read the Bible regularly, a large proportion would argue that those who rely upon the Book for guidance are fooling themselves.

Table 9.3

Firmly-held Religious Beliefs of the Busters

belief statement	strongly agree
• there is only one God and He created the universe and rules it today	66%
• God hears all people's prayers and has the power to answer those prayers	62
• Jesus Christ was God's son who rose from the dead and is alive today	50
• the Bible is the word of God and is totally accurate in all that it teaches	44
• you have a responsibility to tell others, who do not have the same beliefs as you, what you believe	36
• Christians, Jews, Buddhists, Muslims and all others pray to the same god, even though they use different names for that god	33
• The devil, or Satan, is not a living being but is a symbol of evil	33
• all good people will go to heaven when they die	27
• the Christian faith has all the answers to leading a successful life	23
• people who rely upon the Bible for guidance are fooling themselves	9
• the whole idea of sin is outdated	9
• the Ten Commandments are not relevant for people who are alive today	8
• God only loves those people who have earned His love	7
• horoscopes and astrology usually provide an accurate prediction of the future	1

Source: Barna Research Group, Ltd.

The nationwide study of high school juniors reported by Ravitch and Finn provides further insight into the Biblical knowledge of Busters. Interestingly, when it comes to factual knowledge, Busters are better versed in the Bible than they are in classic literature. The tests administered to nearly 8,000 randomly chosen students showed that they were more likely to offer correct answers to multiple-choice queries regarding the Bible than they did in relation to Shakespeare, Greek mythology, and American authors such as Hemingway and Whitman.

Here is what the research showed:

➤ 80% knew that the Biblical account of creation could be found in the book of Genesis.

➤ 78% knew the basic theme of the story of David and Goliath.

➤ 70% knew that Judas was the person who betrayed Jesus Christ.

➤ 67% were able to choose the basic theme of the story of Cain and Abel.

➤ 61% associated Solomon with wisdom.

➤ 60% knew the basic theme of the story of Jonah and the fish.

➤ 57% correctly identified the general content of the tale about the prodigal son.

➤ 37% associated Job with patience.

➤ 33% knew the significance of Sodom and Gomorrah.

It is possible to assume, then, that not only have most Busters been exposed to Judeo-Christian principles and religious experiences, but that their current rejection of the Christian faith is not done in ignorance.

Blame It on Religion

When it comes to influence, the Busters are less likely than are older adults to indicate that religion is losing influence on society. Overall, 37% of the Busters claim that religion has the same degree of influence on society today as it did five years ago. Equal proportions of Busters say that religion has more influence today (29%) as claim it actually has less (29%). By way of comparison, older adults are more likely to view religion as losing its influence on our society.

There is virtually no distinction in the minds of Busters regarding the changing degree of influence of religion and that of Christianity in America.

How can Busters' more optimistic view toward religious influence, in comparison to their elders, be explained? It appears to be related to the underlying assumptions of the population group. Older Americans lived in an era when the impact of churches and religious institutions was more overt and socially acceptable. Busters did not grow up witnessing such an environment. Compared to what they have experienced in the past decade (the only years in which they might have had any discernible sensitivity to the issue), there has been relatively little change as far as they could tell. Never a group to dote on history or precedent, Busters know what they have experienced and little else. Using that limited history as a yardstick, their views are understandable.

On a more personal note, the impact of religious beliefs may be most keenly felt in regard to family realities. Almost half of the Busters (46%) said that their religious beliefs and experiences had "a lot" of impact on their views about family matters. Just 12% stated that their religious beliefs and experiences had exacted no influence over their perspectives on family.

Similarly, nearly half of the Busters (46%) said that their views on marriage have been influenced "a lot" by their religious beliefs and experiences while 15% said these had not influenced their marriage views at all.

With Busters increasingly confronting the realities of raising children, and the statistics showing the unprecedented numbers of Busters experiencing abortions and giving birth outside of marriage, it may be surprising to learn that 37% said their views on raising children have been affected a lot by their religious background. Seventeen percent said religion has not impacted their child-rearing perspectives at all.

As for the most controversial aspect related to intimate relationships—sexual behavior—religious influence is least apparent. Not only did a smaller proportion of Busters concede that their sexual activity has been shaped by their religious training (25%), but an equivalent proportion (22%) noted that their sexual behavior has not been influenced at all by their religious beliefs and experiences.

Grading God's Army

The impressions that Busters hold of religious organizations underscore their reasons for remaining on the sidelines.

Consider, for instance, their impressions of major religious groups. As outlined in Table 9.4, there is only one religious group in America that a majority of Busters have a very favorable impression of—and even that case is not what it appears to be. The Salvation Army, which is a Protestant denomination, is viewed very favorably by six out of ten Busters. However, further research also revealed that a surprisingly small number of them knew it was a church. Many Busters, like older Americans, perceive the Salvation Army to be a social concern ministry, more of a parachurch organization than a local church entity.

Five major religious organizations or movements have a substantially more positive than negative image in the minds of Busters. The Catholic church (30% very favorable, 5% very unfavorable) has the highest strongly favorable rating, trailed by Protestant churches (24%), Baptist churches (20%), Jewish congregations (18%), and Methodist churches (12%).

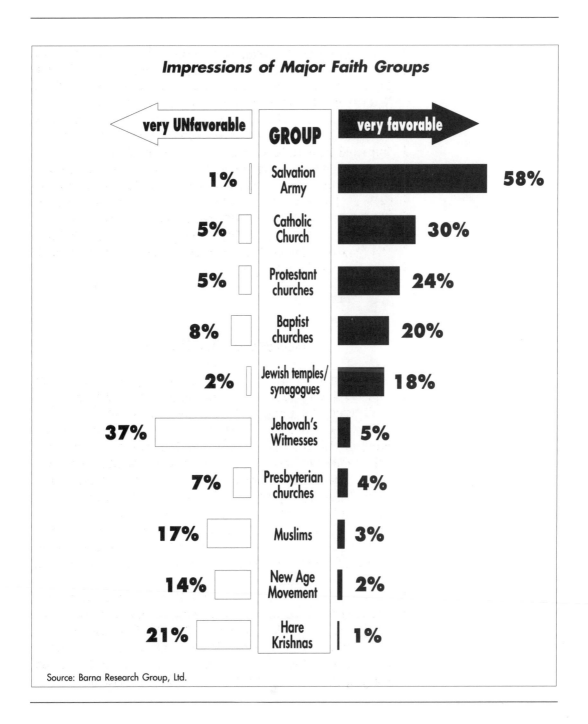

Impressions of Major Faith Groups

very UNfavorable	GROUP	very favorable
1%	Salvation Army	58%
5%	Catholic Church	30%
5%	Protestant churches	24%
8%	Baptist churches	20%
2%	Jewish temples/ synagogues	18%
37%	Jehovah's Witnesses	5%
7%	Presbyterian churches	4%
17%	Muslims	3%
14%	New Age Movement	2%
21%	Hare Krishnas	1%

Source: Barna Research Group, Ltd.

Eight major faith groups were more likely to generate more intensely negative feelings than intensely positive. Those groups include the Mormons, Presbyterians, Lutherans, Jehovah's Witnesses, Hare Krishnas, Muslims, Buddhists, and the New Age Movement.

The other important realization is that Busters possess limited knowledge of most of these groups. Their opinions of such groups tend to be moderate in intensity.

Table 9.4
Impressions of Major Faith Groups

faith group	very favorable	very unfavorable
Salvation Army	58%	1%
Catholic church	30	5
Protestant churches	24	5
Baptist churches	20	8
Jewish temples/synagogues	18	2
Methodist churches	12	8
Mormon churches	3	17
Lutheran churches	7	9
Jehovah's Witnesses	5	37
Presbyterian churches	4	7
Muslims	3	17
Buddhists	3	21
New Age movement	2	14
Hare Krishnas	1	21

Source: Barna Research Group, Ltd.

When Busters evaluate what they have experienced within local churches, there is not a single ministry aspect on which a majority rate churches as doing an "excellent" job. They award the highest marks for the preaching, facilities, congregational friendliness, and concern of the clergy for the people. The lowest grades are given for the teaching, the programs for children, and the teen programs.

Along the same lines, there is not a single people group to whose needs a majority of Busters claim that Protestant churches are very sensitive. The segments to which such churches are deemed most sensitive are families and senior citizens. They are least complimentary regarding Protestant church sensitivity to the needs of men under 35, all minority groups, and single adults. (Remember that the majority of Busters are currently single, and that a higher proportion of Busters than any other generation is comprised of individuals from minority segments.) Less than one out of five Busters said that Protestant churches are very sensitive to the needs of men under 35, men over 35, women under 35, women over 35, teenagers, blacks, hispanics, asians, singles, single parents, and non-Christians.

The Dream Church

What type of church would Busters find most appealing? Based on their stated preferences, they're looking for a church home which would meet the following profile:

➤ 200-300 people

➤ has services at various times throughout the week

➤ meets in a church building

➤ has a male pastor

➤ is associated with a denomination which they find acceptable

➤ emphasizes meeting the needs of the community, rather than focusing upon the needs of the congregation itself or the needs of people overseas

➤ combines both traditional and contemporary church music

Busters, wise in the ways of the world at a young age, prefer a church which has a narrowly defined, articulated sense of purpose. They expect the church to do whatever it does with excellence; nothing less is acceptable. They do not plan to devote much of their free time to the workings of the church or its outreach programs, but expect those programs to be effective and to provide practical life assistance to a variety of people. The services they desire are short, upbeat, professional and non-participatory.

The thrust for practical help is evident when it comes to enumerating those aspects of ministry at which they claim churches have done poorly. Among those areas are avoiding substance abuse; developing leadership skills; developing meaningful relationships with other people; playing a role in peacemaking efforts; knowing how to communicate better with family; and doing better in school.

Marketplace Religion

In the end, Busters maintain a semi-open mind to the potential of religion playing a central role in their life. Their past experiences preclude them from rushing into a long-term, binding relationship with any of the major faith groups of which they are aware. But, given their unfulfilled journey in search of meaning and satisfaction in life, many Busters would give a promising religious entity a hearing.

If religion is to bring hope into people's lives, Busters would describe that hope as it relates to the explication of ethical insight, purpose for living, and the development of greater emotional balance. Their interest in spiritual matters wanes as soon as the discussion rolls around to matters of a higher level; religion, for their purposes, must be tangible, useful and intelligent.

B E H I N D
The Facade

Lisa Baker ◆ Age: 20

"I grew up in a very religious home. My parents made us go to mass every Sunday. Once I turned 18, that was it. I haven't been back to the Catholic church since. I have visited a bunch of other churches, to see what they're about. It's been interesting, but I still haven't found the answer."

Lisa, like many of her generation, is still searching for "the answer." Disenchanted with much of what life has thrust in her path, she is seeking understanding about her purpose, about the reason for pain and suffering, and for the answers to other challenging questions.

"When I find a place that can really answer those questions, I'll want to be a part of what they are doing. I'm not against churches or religion. I just don't want to waste my time in places that have no real wisdom, only to discover that when I'm 50 or something."

The New Age is strangely appealing to her. *"I don't go for the wacked out stuff—the crystals and all. But the philosophy is good: harmony with the universe, peace with yourself and others, striving for a higher purpose. But it's not really something you can get your hands on.*

It's too fuzzy. It probably has some truth to it, but I don't know if the New Age religions provide the real answers."

The mainstream faiths have been a disappointment to her. "I honestly tried them. They just couldn't speak to me."

> **"I don't go for the wacked out stuff—the crystals and all. But the philosophy is good: harmony with the universe, peace with yourself and others..."**

She harangues them for being "irrelevant, boring, so old." But she does not preclude the possibility of someday winding up back in a Catholic or even a Protestant church.

"All I want is reality. Show me God. Tell me what He is really like. Help me to understand why life is the way it is, and how I can experience it more fully and with greater joy. I don't want the empty promises. I want the real thing. And I'll go wherever I find that truth system."

TEN

Making the Most of the Journey

I T IS VIRTUALLY INEVITABLE THAT YOU WILL HAVE SERIOUS interaction with Busters in the future. Practically speaking, given that they are almost seventy million strong, there is no avoiding them. More importantly, there is no reason to avoid them.

As you encounter Busters, remember that they view and respond to the world differently than the rest of America does. Here are some thoughts on how to maximize your relationships with them—whether it be a work, personal, or mentoring relationship.

From the Heart

One of the driving forces among Busters is to retain a sense of dignity through autonomy. They do not have the same social righteousness of the Boomers in the late Sixties, but they do possess a desire to make their feelings, beliefs and presence felt in significant ways. They are not willing to sit back and accept whatever the Boomers, Builders and Seniors define as right or wrong, as the new realities.

It is helpful to remember and quickly disarm their natural skepticism about older people. This is often accomplished by allowing Busters the opportunity to make their views known and to hear a lucid explanation of why things will be done a certain way. They are an idiosyncratic group, and part of the challenge to working with them successfully is to comprehend their individual quirks and unusual expectations toward leading them or teaming with them in productive ways.

Busters have a unique blend of personality traits. Many are outgoing but skeptical, curious but defensive, willing listeners but weak communicators. Interacting with Busters may take more time and skill than one is used to providing. The danger is to assume that they are operating from the same basic assumptions and values as everyone else. Don't make such an assumption.

> "Deep down, a majority of Busters struggle with feelings of alienation. They feel estranged from family, from community, from God, and often from self."

Deep down, a majority of Busters struggle with feelings of alienation. They feel estranged from family, from community, from God, and often from self. It is an ugly place to be, emotionally. Busters are determined to overcome the nausea created by this relational malaise. If you are aware of their desire to connect more deeply with their environment at the same time that they are critically evaluating the value systems and expectations of others whom they encounter, you may be better able to strike a responsive chord or achieve a deeper relational balance with Busters.

Whether it is instinctive or defensive, they tend to want more meaningful relationships in their lives. Those relationships must be built around their emotional parameters, though. Pessimism and cynical perspectives may be a part of their natural response to stimuli. These are not necessarily their perceptual judgments on the individuals with whom they come in contact; it is more likely a defense mechanism to withstand the deprivation they expect to encounter.

In their continuing search for a more permanent, viable value system, expect to encounter what seem like inconsistent behaviors and perspectives from Busters. They are probably not lying to you when they change their tune; more likely, they are testing a new approach to making reality fit together. The best response to such inconsistencies is not to call them on the inconsistency, but to gracefully challenge how the latest view they have expressed fits within the prior perspectives to which they had alluded. As much as anything, Busters need the chance to work through the process of arriving at a workable value system, without being chastised for working through the process.

Given one of their underlying assumptions about reality—i.e. that all truth is relative—their world view and their moral imperatives may change frequently or appear to be internally contradictory. Realize that they are in a transition mode and require some slack. In all likelihood, they would appreciate some guidance in their explorations—as long as it is not rigid and self-righteous.

Those who claim to possess absolute truth almost automatically lose their credibility in the eyes of Busters. They are skeptical of the person's motives and wisdom. Those who believe they possess truth would be well-advised not merely to proclaim it (Busters do maintain that talk is cheap) but to demonstrate it in real, rather than conceptual or theoretical, ways.

Busters on the Job

Employers have quite a challenge when it comes to enabling Busters both to fit with the prevailing corporate culture and to realize their own potential.

Appealing to tradition, to the importance of history, or to respect for age will fall on deaf or even hostile ears. The keys to the working life, for Busters, are positive, tangible outcomes: financial rewards, career mobility, educational options or achievement, and significant relationships. Jobs and occupational involvement which allow for personal development and corporate achievement while moving toward such tangible outcomes will serve to motivate the Busters—for as long as they remain interested in the job, the people, and the tasks at hand. Their decisions about such matters may appear to change as quickly and unpredictably as the wind.

Try not to be turned off by their pessimism or their constant questioning of authority and decisions. Their intent is not to undermine; they simply believe they have something to offer and are trying to gain a toehold in a world which they believe has left them out of the game.

Employers have found that developing a team approach works better with Busters than does an authoritarian, vertical management structure. Not only does a team environment facilitate their involvement in the decision-making process, it also gives them more of the sense of community they are seeking.

This strategy may be especially important when Busters are expected to work with (or for) Boomers. The innate distrust or distaste Busters have for Boomers is sometimes uncontainable. Working in a horizontal rather than vertical authority structure may reduce some of the tensions that might otherwise emerge.

The Boomers who have successfully worked with Busters have been those who held a clearly articulated, shared vision for the future. Focused on that joint understanding of the ends, the process was enhanced by providing Busters with the perpetual opportunity to discuss new courses of action and a variety of approaches to completing the tasks at hand. Boomers who wish to control Busters by lines of authority—a natural tendency for the control-driven Boomer generation—will find that they will attract few Busters as allies or complacent colleagues.

> **"And don't be shocked when you review people's attendance records and find that Busters have taken additional days off, beyond their paid vacation time. Leisure time is more important to them than work."**

Understand what makes the Busters uncomfortable. For instance, practices such as long-term planning raise their anxiety levels. Emphasis upon a future determined for them is likely to increase their stress levels because they experience a loss of control over their own destiny. Already skittish about the future and their role in it, such a close encounter with plans designed to nail down their world for them may raise anger or ambivalence about further involvement with the people or process.

Busters are likely to approve of organizations which offer them valuable on-the-job training. Overall, of course, their primary interest is to understand what they, personally, will gain from involvement at the company or in a particular task. This is one of the characteristics they probably absorbed from Boomers. Their value system is different, though, so they are seeking a divergent set of rewards for their performance. Giving them training is often seen as a major benefit, one which can motivate greater loyalty and commitment to their job.

The danger in investing in Busters, however, is that they will take the training and convert it into a higher paying, more responsible job with a competitor. There may be value to structuring such training in return for promises of longer-term employment with the company.

Indeed, a company that is consistently aware of and concerned about the career development and success of the Buster will have a more productive and satisfied employee on its hands. While this is generally true for all employees, regardless of their generation, the condition is exaggerated among Busters. It is helpful to spend more time with Busters, reaching a common understanding of where things are at and where they are headed so that Busters know their importance to the company. Such intimacy also protects the company from unexpected or surprise changes of career in which the loss of the Buster could put the company at a disadvantage.

And don't be shocked when you review people's attendance records and find that Busters have taken additional days off, beyond their paid vacation time. Leisure time is more important to them than work. In fact, to motivate Busters, offering additional time off, rather than extra pay, often serves as a more powerful incentive. Experience suggests that the more fulfilling the job becomes—relationally, more than productively—the less additional time off they will take.

Pushing them to greater productivity levels generally cannot be accomplished by resorting to negative challenges: "I bet you can't do this." That stoked the competitive fires of many a Boomer. Busters, though, see such challenges as insults or condemnations; it is merely further evidence that their character is being questioned and their future being determined for them. Their likely response will be to excuse themselves from the game; a take-my-ball-and-go-home reaction.

Neither should an employer expect that Busters will invest more of themselves in a job than is absolutely necessary. The workaholic tendencies of the Boomers will not be replicated by the Busters. If you will need extra hours to complete a special task, think of creative ways to get the job done. Asking Busters to put in more time will generally be greeted with a "you must be kidding" attitude.

In fact, Busters seem to take little, if any, pride in their work. They do have pride in their efforts, but they get their joy not so much from accomplishing corporate productivity or profit goals so much as believing that what they are doing has a larger benefit, either personal or societal. Busters put their skills to good use especially when their efforts have a synergistic impact, through team cooperation that achieves a common goal of positive impact.

Communicating effectively with Busters is often enhanced by the use of video-based presentations. They were weaned on video images and tend to see their world in light of how television and the movies have portrayed reality. Interspersing video and PC-driven communications with personal interaction can offer both the creative stimuli and varied inputs that cause them to get involved. Because their attention spans are shorter and they are more responsive to creative and colorful messages, restructuring the training and reporting environment to provide video-driven messages may prove to be more beneficial.

The Spiritual Journey

As in the other dimensions of their lives, the spiritual journey of Busters is based upon a desire to grow personally through the discovery of personally beneficial truths and practices. What most churches and religious organizations fail to offer is a tangible means of becoming a more completely whole individual. The religious faiths that will win the support of the Busters are those which enhance relationships and lifestyles.

The spiritual quest of the Busters is not a dimension to be taken lightly. In their search for meaning and fulfillment, there is an underlying assumption that religion may hold part of the answer. Their expectation is that it is possible to intertwine aspects of religious insight with the perceptual filter (or in some cases, philosophy of life) which they possess. As someone divulges insights which are relevant and smack of excellence, the Busters will pay attention and will splice that which they perceive to be of value onto their existing core of beliefs.

Allowing a faith to be positioned as a series of rules, traditions or punishments is antithetical to the search of the Busters. Their need is for a system which will enlighten them, a means of clarifying and distinguishing what is ultimately useful and true from that which is superfluous and meaningless. A faith that becomes positioned as a means of growing personally through deeper relationships and understanding would be more attractive.

Busters have little understanding of some of the core values of the Christian faith, such as worship. Ministering to them requires a special balance of sensitivity to what they do and do not know. They have been exposed to enough Christian teaching that they feel they know what it is all about. Yet, they do not have a deep enough grasp of the faith to mentally piece together the big picture of Christianity, and what that faith might do for them. Consequently, they take bits and pieces of various faiths and blend them together into a personalized, customized brand of religion. They may call it Christianity, but it is not an orthodox brand of the faith.

Expecting the personal faith of Busters to result in social activism may be expecting too much at this stage of their lives. While they are touched with feelings of compassion for the poor and the emotionally hurting, they are not driven to respond personally. They would be more likely to take a stand on issues such as substance abuse, illiteracy, urban or ethnic animosity, and environmental protection. But even on these issues, tying a religious belief system to social activism would be a tough sell. If the outreach efforts can become positioned as a group experience that leaves a positive mark on the world, the chances of energizing Buster involvement would be enhanced.

The Days Ahead

Just as working with the Boomers was a strange and often frustrating experience for employers, religious leaders and policymakers in the late Sixties and in the Seventies, so will activating Busters be a true challenge. Making it work for everyone will require a new set of insights into the minds and hearts of this searching generation.

Make no mistake about it, though; the Busters are here to stay and will definitely influence the value system and approach to life of the American people. To continue to ignore them is to invite disaster. To work with them on the basis of assumptions culled from experiences with the Boomers will result in problems. The task at hand is to know them, to love them and to work in cooperation with them to achieve a more viable society that reflects a compassionate, growing people.

Appendices

APPENDIX ONE

Data Cited in This Book

Throughout this book various charts and tables appear which cite the Barna Research Group, Ltd. as the source. Each of those tables and charts depicts information drawn from studies conducted by the Barna Research Group (BRG), an independent marketing research company based in Glendale, California. The studies were conducted among nationwide, representative samples of adults. The adults were interviewed anonymously by telephone on weekday evenings or during the day on weekends.

Those individuals were chosen through the use of a sampling technique known as "random-digit dialing" (RDD). This is a means by which a computer generates telephone numbers to be called by the research company's interviewers. The telephone numbers themselves may or may not be working numbers. The advantages of using an RDD sample, as opposed to selecting numbers from a telephone book, are myriad. Perhaps chief among them is greater inclusivity (i.e. all telephone households are equally likely to be called, even if they have new or unlisted numbers).

The studies from which data were drawn were conducted in 1990, 1991 and 1992. The sample sizes ranged from 1,002 to 1,500, all respondents being 18 or older (unless otherwise noted). In some cases, due to the use of the same question with an equivalent sample universe and the same data collection methodology, data were added from two or more surveys conducted within a twelve-month period. This had the effect of increasing the aggregate sample size and decreasing the estimated sampling error.

The data presented regarding Baby Busters represents a slice of the aggregate survey data collected. Thus, in a survey of 1,500 people, we would generally interview approximately 250 Busters.

Additional studies were referenced which had been conducted among younger respondents (13-18 years of age). In those studies, the entire base of respondents was included among those individuals who were referred to as Busters. When their responses were added to those of older Busters, the ages of the respondents were statistically weighted to provide a balanced perspective of the Buster reality.

APPENDIX TWO

- American Chicle Group. *American Chicle Youth Poll.* New York: Warner-Lambert Company. 1987.

- Astin, Alexander W., William S. Korn, Ellyne R. Berz. *The American Freshman: National Norms for Fall 1980.* Los Angeles: Cooperative Institutional Research Program, UCLA. 1980.

- —— *The American Freshman: National Norms for Fall 1990.* Los Angeles: Cooperative Institutional Research Program, UCLA. 1990.

- Bachman, Jerald, Lloyd D. Johnston, and Patrick M. O'Malley. *Monitoring the Future: Questionnaire Responses From the Nation's High School Seniors.* Ann Arbor: Institute for Social Research. 1986.

- Barna, George. *The Barna Report 1992-93.* Ventura, CA: Regal Books. 1992.

- —— *Today's Teens: A Generation in Transition.* Glendale, CA: Barna Research Group. 1990.

- —— *What Americans Believe.* Ventura, CA: Regal Books. 1991.

- Bradford, Lawrence J. and Claire Raines. *Twentysomething: Managing and Motivating Today's New Work Force.* New York: MasterMedia Ltd. 1992.

- Bureau of the Census. *Statistical Abstracts of the United States.* Washington, DC: Bureau of the Census. 1991.

- Littwin, Susan. *The Postponed Generation: Why American Youth are Growing Up Later.* New York: William Morrow & Co. 1986.

- Ravitch, Diane and Chester Finn, Jr. *What Do Our 17-Year-Olds Know?* New York: Perennial Library. 1988.

- Search Institute. *Effective Christian Education: A National Study of Protestant Congregations.* Minneapolis, MN: Search Institute. 1990.

Appendix Three

About the Barna Research Group, Ltd.

The Barna Research Group (BRG) was launched in 1984 by George and Nancy Barna. The firm has grown steadily since that time, emerging as a full-service research team that provides assistance to a broad range of clients. Their past clients have included Visa; The Disney Channel; World Vision; CBN; Rapp Collins Marcoa; J. Walter Thompson Advertising; Billy Graham Evangelistic Association; Focus on the Family; *Bookstore Journal;* Word Books; *Non-Profit Times;* and a host of others.

BRG offers services related to project design, questionnaire development, data collection and tabulation, data analysis, focus groups, in-depth interviewing, data presentations, and other specialized research services.

Other Resources from BRG

In addition, BRG produces many information resources for use by organizations, especially churches and Christian ministries. Among the currently available resources are the following.

Newsletter:

- *Ministry Currents: Perspectives on Ministry in an Era of Change*

Books (by George Barna):

- *The Barna Report, 1992-1993*
- *What Americans Believe*
- *The Frog in the Kettle*
- *A Step by Step Guide to Church Marketing*
- *User Friendly Churches*
- *The Future of the American Family*

Reports:

- *Never on a Sunday: The Challenge of the Unchurched*
- *Today's Teens: A Generation in Transition*
- *Sources of Information for Ministry and Business*

BRG is also a qualified re-marketer of several secondary databases, including the 1990 Census.

If you would like to get more information about the Barna Research Group, available resources, or to discuss the possibility of conducting a research project with BRG, please write or call.

Barna Research Group, Ltd.
647 W. Broadway • Glendale, CA 91204
818-241-9300 • fax 818-246-7684

Thank You

Thanks to our Buster stand-ins: Gabe, Carlos, Kevin, Billy, Scot, Maggie, Mike, Vibeke, Gary, and Jacki, whose portraits helped illustrate this look at the Buster generation.